MASCULINE MYTHS

.....HIGH TIME TO DISCLOSE

MUGDHA VERMA

Copyright © Mugdha Verma
All Rights Reserved.

This book has been published with all efforts taken to make the material error-free after the consent of the author. However, the author and the publisher do not assume and hereby disclaim any liability to any party for any loss, damage, or disruption caused by errors or omissions, whether such errors or omissions result from negligence, accident, or any other cause.

While every effort has been made to avoid any mistake or omission, this publication is being sold on the condition and understanding that neither the author nor the publishers or printers would be liable in any manner to any person by reason of any mistake or omission in this publication or for any action taken or omitted to be taken or advice rendered or accepted on the basis of this work. For any defect in printing or binding the publishers will be liable only to replace the defective copy by another copy of this work then available.

This book is dedicated to the shrewd-minded women around us who have misused the laws and have harassed true and naive men.

The astute-minded girls are the ones who are my inspiration to write this book.

I believe that necessity is the mother of all inventions, and because of their actions, soon the law will understand to have a relook at the existing laws and can think to create some laws in favour of the neglected gender too.

Contents

FOREWORD

AIl INDIA COUNCIL OF HUMAN RIGHTS LIBERTIES AND SOCIAL JUSTICE
Authorized Signatory member of
(UNITED NATIONS GLOBAL COMPACT)

DR. ANTONY RAJU

Advocate - Supreme Court
Founder President

FOREWORD

To write against the established practice and system is not only challenging but also a test of one's own endurance. The writer has come forward at a time when our society is undergoing a vast sea of cyclical changes. And we all read in newspapers about the misuse of laws which were once framed to protect women against the atrocities of patriarchal abuses.

That is true for long-time women who were on the wrong side of our matrimonial institution and were actual sufferers of the atrocities faced after marriage. However, in today's world it is exactly the opposite, i.e., men now face the heat of matrimonial discord as much as women. In fact, the number of cases related to divorce has increased manifold after the Corona pandemic. The writer has substantiated her claims by showing the real statistics.

Once again, the ball is in the court to decide on certain amendments to such laws that will make the environment more breathable. Still, the common man has not lost faith in the temple of justice. The writer has put down a reason for the judiciary to look on the other side of such laws.

I wish the book would provide a suitable connecting link among the various affected families, be it a doctor, an engineer, a bureaucrat, a shopkeeper, any professional, etc., to unite for an unbiased society. There is no better time as this to launch this book on such a critical social issue lest a need is felt to bring out a manual of code of conduct on "Post marital life".

Wish you all the best,

Dr. Anthony Raju 8/7/22

HEAD OFFICE ADDRESS
C-1088/1, Ward No : 1, 1st Floor, Above Suresh Electronics, Near Gurudwara Mehrauli, New Delhi - 110030 Mob : 98730 87903 | 98730 05424
Email : humanrightscouncil.org@gmail.com office@humanrightscouncil.in / Visit : www.humanrightscouncil.in | www.newsindiatoday.tv

Good Wishes

While many books have been written related to problems faced by women and are well recognised by many social awareness movements as well as support groups and legislation, it takes a lot of courage to talk about the opposite-where men are exploited by women and our systems remain biased both by societal beliefs and legal systems. I congratulate Mugdha Verma for taking up this issue, which is considered taboo, through her book titled "Masculine Myths", she has used a conversational storytelling style and mixed facts and fiction to convey her message through this book in an engrossing manner.

Over the last two decades or so, we've kept hearing stories from family and friends about how these situations are much more common than one would believe. In one case, someone who is known me since childhood was faced with a situation where a case against him was filed by his daughter-in-law for torture, forced abortion, etc. Fortunately for him, his son had kept the pregnancy test (showing a negative result) and other pieces of evidence that helped them get out of the tricky situation. As details emerged later, all of this was a way to blackmail him to share part of his retirement funds! The pace at which false cases are being registered in courts against men is astonishing and can be very easily compared to a fatal disease such as gangrene.

The author also quotes how the male suicide index has increased, and in particular, the husband suicide index over the last 20 years. This is an alarming situation and would have an impact on our marriage and family system as well as our social fabric.

Mugdha tries her best to show the other side of the coin and the existing truth of a society where males are being suppressed. She speaks out loud for justice towards the suffering individual's being gender unbiased. I would mark this book as rare because, to date, very few people have dared touch upon a topic that is and will always be argumentative and who to consider right or wrong.

This book will give you a realistic feel and some real stories of the social evil happening in our society but being hidden under wraps and veils. I am thankful to the author of this book for being the torch bearer to create awareness among the masses by writing and narrating in a common man's language.

I wish Mugdha the best of luck and hope that this book is read by a large portion of society and that it leads to appropriate changes in our social and legal systems to make it gender neutral so that an innocent person is treated as innocent until proven guilty!

Prof. Prabhat RANJAN,
ViceChancellor DY Patil International University
(DYPIU)
(Former ED, TIFAC)

<u>Good Wishes</u>

This book draws attention to the tyranny of law; law that is unequally loaded to the side of one gender. All laws are necessarily made to address injustices to a large set of citizens. When a set of laws fails the test of equality and balance, the set becomes prone to abuse, misuse and injustice to another set of citizens.

The writer has made a bold attempt to highlight the infirmities of laws meant to protect women from male tyranny in a patriarchal society. Being herself a woman, she has used her perch position to highlight the hijacking of well intentioned laws by unscrupulous women. No doubt, many cases under these laws are now falling through the judicial process.

While it is no one's case for repeal of any of these laws, amendments to protect the constitutional rights of the accused will provide sharper teeth to these laws and enhance the interests of women.

I am confident that Mugdha's initiative will engender more debate, research and efforts to make these women-centric laws more effective and just to ensure social, familial and domestic harmony in matrimony.

I commend Mugdha's calling out of the tyranny of these laws. May her singular voice in this book create resounding thunders for reforms!

Vidya Bhushan
Retd. General Manager, East Coast Railway (ECoR)

PREFACE

Everything created in the world was designed to meet the needs of every human being, whether they were materialistic or provided under the protection of the law. And surprisingly, everything that a human being received in excess was exploited to its max. Anything in excess is bad, and the same is very clear with the women oriented laws, which are actually made to help the needy naive women who are truly being harassed by the opposite gender. However, the true benefits are reaped by the astute-minded smart women who understand how to leverage the opportunity to their advantage.

The word "feminism" is a sentiment associated with many men and women. For women, it is obvious to hold it as it helps them to achieve equality among the sexes, be it social, political, economic, or personal. It is a tool for granting women the right to stand equal to every other gender in society. It was brought up as a noble idea for a noble cause. But every implication has its pros and cons. While I was growing up, I could see the hidden side of feminism. If some people wisely try to analyse the things going around them, it will not be difficult for them to assess the injustice that has started flourishing towards a single gender again. History has started

repeating itself, only the roles have been interchanged. Earlier, women were the victims of men, and now it has become common that men are the victims of women. Everything happening is not well justified under the shadow of "feminism", as it was supposed to be. As every coin has two sides, similarly, "feminism" has both angelic and demonic sides to it. The angelic side is very good and is made to benefit the girls who are the real sufferers, whereas the demonic side includes those females who start using it to achieve their personal benefit, e.g., to take personal revenge, satisfy their ego, to dominate on the other sex, to extort money and a lot more. As we say, with every good there is evil. So, it is with "feminism". It has made many men cry bloody tears. It has ruined many happy families and has snatched away their happiness. Being selfish is good, but make sure that your self-love does not end up making you a despot, someone who has a lot of power and uses it cruelly and unreasonably.

Surprisingly, we can find feminist men and women who support women at every step of their lives, but alas, it's rare to find women who are meninists and support men. As we humans are social animals, we need each other's support for survival, and it is the right of every species on earth to survive with pride and peace, but it has been taken over only by the female. It is surprising to see that men are being suppressed and are always considered wrong for every act done on earth. It feels guilty when we see an innocent man suffering. Emotions must be equal for every gender. Our mindsets have become so rigid since the inception of this world that we always consider men wrong. For instance, let us assume that you find a girl beating a guy on the street. What thought will hit your mind first? Definitely, you all will feel that the guy must have done something wrong. And what do you think if you see a woman beaten up by a guy? Then you all will pity the girl and curse the boy for being spineless and senseless for not respecting women. Nobody will ever try to put effort into thinking the opposite way.

The very popular real-life incident, "The Lucknow Road Rage Incident," captures the true spirit of my above concern, where a woman was seen thrashing a man and his phone in front of the public. To my surprise, people were gathered, not to offer any help to the man, but instead to capture the incident. After committing the heinous crime, the lady had the courage to falsify the story and register a complaint against the innocent man. Soon, he was arrested and was sent to jail. But maybe his stars were in his favour and the incident took place where the CCTV was installed, and it was very clear from the footage that the female was the one to be blamed for the incident.

The power which was shown by the lady was not of her own rather it was the 'gifted power' by the law, which is handy for women to carry misconduct with whom so ever she wishes without even thinking twice. The violence which she was carrying was not coming to an end and her ego was not getting satisfied even afterslapping the cab driver more than 20 times and crushing his phone too. Then why are men always considered violent and cruel?

Actually, the law has created a bulwark for the crime committed by the women in the name of self- protection. In the time of equality, why is the law biased towards the women considering them the weaker sex. The weaker sex should be called to the one who are vulnerable, unprotected, defenseless, helpless, open, at-risk irrespective of the gender. I am sure that if there would have been no CCTV as proof, the man would have to suffer throughout his life, even now he might have to suffer the lifelong mental agony which is hard to compensate.

It is my tiny attempt to make people aware of the hidden trauma which is being faced by the innocent men community ending up their life after getting caught in the demonic feminist shadow. It is high time for every species to think about the well-being of everybody around them irrespective of the gender. There should be a war, not between men and women, but between right and wrong. I would request you all to become selfish and start raising your voice against the erroneous act to protect yourself because it is not far when demonic feminism will engulf everyone becoming gender unbiased.

Acknowledgements

Writing a book is harder than I thought and more rewarding than I could have ever imagined. If this book is a success, I owe all my gratitude to the people surrounding me, who have put effort into it to help me complete my dream project of writing this book.

I also owe my gratitude to my great grandfather, the late Sh. Jaganmohan Verma, an editor of Hindi Shabd Sagar. He had an unequalled contribution to the creation of Hindi Shabdsagar. He has penned many books and has translated a Chinese book written by Fa-Hien into Hindi "Chini Yatri Fahiyan Ka Yatra-Vivaran". I am truly blessed and grateful to him for genetically transferring to me his zeal for writing books.

It would not have been possible without the help of the strong pillars of my life, the reason for my life, my mother Jyotsna, and father Buddha Prakash Verma. Asking my father to go through the book several times a day and night and getting input and feedback from him was truly blissful. I would like to acknowledge the extraordinary debt I owe to my parents, who gave me an upbringing wherein I think in an unbiased manner and prefer to stand on the truth only.

Some people are always there for you
through thick and thin. They silently support you and constantly motivate you. I know I will always have a back to lie on. I am indebted to my elder brother, Rahul, for the immense support he has given me at every stage of my life. In a crowd, if I can see someone cheering for me. I can blindly guess that it's you, my brother.

I am very grateful to my husband, Kshitij, as the main reason behind the birth of this book is him. Writing a book with a kid around you is very difficult, but I could do it just because of him. He managed my elder kid, Mrigasya, so that I could finish my book. Right from the start, he made him eat, bathe, took him out, and put him to sleep so that I could get ample alone time to think and write the book. My partner has gone to great lengths to manage my child so that I can think and write. Along with my first kid, he took care of me too, as I was pregnant while creating this book. This book is my third baby. My eldest son also made sure not to disturb me when I was putting my thoughts into this book. My youngest baby, DakshIvaan, also cooperated a lot while in the womb. He never kicked or disturbed me during my writing time. My kids are my inspiration and the reason for all my efforts. I am truly blessed to have my life partner beside me who is my source of inspiration, my motivation, my encouragement. I made him read the book each day with whatever I was adding to the book, even if it was late at night.

I am thankful to my friend Kanchana, a lawyer by profession, for encouraging me to write and finish this book.

I pay my gratitude to the 16th president of the USA, Mr. Abraham Lincoln, as his quote "nearly all men can stand adversity, but if you want to test a man's character, give him power" inspired me a lot to come up with the hidden fact and the other side of the coin. I read it as and I rephrased this quote as "nearly all women can stand adversity, but if you want to test a woman's character, give her the power of the law".

I am grateful to the people of society. Although we haven't yet met, we are all in some way related to each other, and we may not meet throughout our lives either. I am thankful to the millions of people around the world who have helped me to write this novel. The present situation happening around the world has helped me to get connected with you all. You all are my indirect influences and motivation to come up with this book. Many people have written books on feminism, but the majority don't bother to look at the other side of the coin. The balance is maintained with both the wheels. Life will not move if there is only one, and everyone should understand this and start worrying about the other aspect too. I tried to keep myself in each person's shoes, who are the real sufferers and going through the pain despite gender. I am always going to be fond of you all as you are all associated with the creation of my first book.

This one's for you all.

With the contributions of you all, we can bring about the required change.

This book is dedicated to many who were martyred by being dragged into the fight in wedlock and were forced to lose their precious lives due to the false accusations made against them.

The pain they had, the pain that is still with their family, can never be understood, but I want to salute them for bearing the pain and the struggles that they had for which they were forced to commit suicide.

Let's make life breathable for all!

I

"Think before making castles in the air. Be aware. Life is unpredictable."

Yes, today I am a poor and helpless lady. You read that right. I haven't been like this since my childhood; rather, I was a very chirpy, happy go-lucky kind of girl. My parents loved me the most of my siblings. I was the most obedient, calm girl and loved to be loved by everyone, be it my parents, relatives, friends, teachers, or whomsoever knew me. We were three siblings, and I was the eldest of all. Mummy always referred to me as the wisest of all. They both used to have a lot of fights, and I was always away from them. I was the only one to resolve their fight. I loved watching movies and was very happy in my own dreamy world. I had big aspirations and big dreams to achieve. I never liked to get into a brawl with them; rather, I loved to help Mummy with her household chores. I remember her telling me, "Your in-laws will be happy with you. They will be the lucky ones to get you. " I cherished my childhood days as everyone pampered me and I loved being showered in the rain of love and pampering.

Wise men have correctly stated that time does not stop for you, no matter how much you want to cling to that moment. It just passes by, leaving you with sweet memories to be cherished for the rest of your life.

It was my first day of school. Mom got me ready, and I stepped into the world of learning. My teachers made me the most pampered student in my class because of my dimples and sweet innocent face. Be it any function in school, I was the one who was chosen by the teachers to welcome the chief guests. I was blessed with a dimpled, charming look and an obedient attitude with a sharp brain. Time went by and I finished my schooling, getting myself ready for the second phase of my life, which was college life. I blossomed and was in my teens. When I entered college, I got a huge fan following. I liked being loved and cherished by many people around me. Every girl must have gone through this phase, and it gives you a different kind of feeling when you are at the start of your college life. You also like to respond to them, not because of the sacraments you are taught, but because you are a teen. But being an Indian girl and because of your upbringing in a family of high virtues, you don't dare take any further steps. Although at this age your heart will start growing wings to fly out and reach the one with whom you may have an infatuation, you will prefer to cut them before they grow further and fly away just because you are taught by your parents not to get into such things as these are the spoilers in life. I was always told in my mind that my parents would search for my prince charming for me, who would take care of me and be my strongest pillar (strength) throughout my life. I believed my parents more than anything else in the world. I remember my father saying to me, "I haven't bowed in front of anybody till date; don't ever let my head go down".

The college days went by, and now I was ready to enter the next phase of my life. Every child feels that their parents are the best, but I felt as if mine were the best among the rest. They were both so supportive and were my angel guides. They always taught me to be strong and to stand on my feet. They always taught me to fight for myself, my rights, and my happiness, as it is the truth of the world that no one will ever come to offer you your happiness. You only have to struggle and fight for yourself. Since I was a girl, I was always taught to gather strength and learn to fight, as you all know what being a girl means to society. You will be undergoing gender discrimination; we are the ones who will have to balance work and life in this so-called modern era too. Stepping out of the house is a horrendous thought for any girl, and stepping out, especially at night, is just beyond our imagination as the vulture eyes will all be around to eat us up if they get the opportunity. We can't even wear what we wish, as the scanners will scan you inside out. This feeling makes us feel very uncomfortable.

Even Mahatma Gandhi once said in 1921: "Of all the evils for which man has made himself responsible, none is so degrading, so shocking or as brutal as his abuse of the better half of humanity, the female sex (not the weaker sex)."

After finishing college, I got a very highly paid job offer. When I discussed it with my parents, they both supported me and were happy with my achievement. I feel so blessed to have such supportive parents in my life who have always shown me the right path and have always helped me make the right decisions. I have never failed in any of the work that I did under their guidance. They are the reason behind my being a strong woman and making my own decisions.

When my parents passed this news to my grandmother, she immediately opposed the idea of me working. She said, "Till she was getting degrees, it was okay but now you guys will get the girl to do the job. Now that such days have come, get your girl to work and live on her money. In our days, we never used to get girls to work outside the house."

But my father interrupted, saying, "What's wrong with it? My girl is no less than a boy."

My grandmother started murmuring, "Do as you feel. I have never seen her prepare a single cup of tea until this day, and now you are not even teaching her to cook, but rather encouraging her to do the job. What is she going to do at her in-laws' house?"

My father shouted in frustration, "Why will my daughter do anything there? She will have maids and servants to do everything for her. You don't worry. I have my daughter and, being her father, I will decide what is going to be good for her."

My grandmother grumbled, "What will you do when she has to listen to her in-laws' taunts?"

My father replied, "I am proud of my daughter and I am sure nothing of this kind will ever happen to her as they will get an earning daughter-in-law."

After the heated argument, there was a deep silence in the room, but there was a tsunami happening within my mom. How can a mother who has given birth to her daughter tolerate all this about her? Even though my *daadi* loved me a lot, I could not love her back, as since childhood I have heard from my mom what she did to her when she entered the home as a new bride and so on in her life till date. I always hated her for not being good to my mom.

I don't know why my dad was so affectionate towards his mother, although she never showed concern towards my mother. She was only concerned about her son and granddaughters and grand sons. This kind of discrimination was never liked by me toward my mother, as my mother is the best and I am so lucky to have a mother like her. How much she cares for her children, how dedicated she is to us. She has to bear so much pain just to bring us up. Although she did not get a healthy environment and was subjected to persistent trauma given by my *daadi*, she made it a point to give us a healthy environment to grow in. I can't even imagine my life without her. I love her possessiveness, which she shows to me, and we also love showering her with our love.

We are three siblings: two sisters and one brother. I was very close to both of them. Imagining my life without them always made me feel down. My siblings were like my lifelines. Whenever I start earning, I could never see them get upset about anything and will try to fulfil all of their dreams. Now that the day has arrived, I can establish myself and become self-dependent to fulfil all my wishes.

III

Since I was grown up enough in the eyes of my relatives, they all started to pester my parents to find a suitable match for me, and it is really surprising to see your parents get caught in their trap. I wanted to live and enjoy my life alone for at least a few years, so I thought I would go and discuss it with my mom. I went to her and put my head on her lap and said, "Mummy, it's very early. I don't want to get married now."

My mom replied, trying to make me understand, "Dear, it's the best time to get married. You will have enough time to enjoy your life with your life partner. Dear, I know that you love to visit places, eat in top restaurants, wear brand-named clothes, and have a good lifestyle. Keeping all that in mind, I will search for the best match for you who will earn at least ten times what you earn so that you can live your life in queen style, my princess, "and she then kissed me on the forehead.

Surprisingly, I asked her, "Really mommy, is it so good to get married? Do we get to have all these things and will I be blessed to have a rich spouse for me?"

She replied, "Of course, darling, you are our daughter and I am not going to throw you away to anybody. We have never made our children compromise for anything in life, and I will make sure that you do not even have to make compromises further in your life too. "

Marriage is fun, which I have felt since my childhood. I had seen my cousins and relatives getting married. It used to be so much fun. Everyone was around the bride to take care of her, and she used to get all the attention with a bunch of new beautiful dresses, so many pieces of jewellery, make-up, and a lot of stuff. I even started imagining myself as beautiful as a princess as a bride in my marriage. All such thoughts caused the fluttering of butterflies in my stomach. It gave me a good feeling. And thus, I never interrupted my parents in doing their task of finding me my soul mate, and thus another part of my story began from here.

My parents were looking for a good match for me and even started purchasing pieces of jewellery for me, as my mom always believed in the proverb 'haste makes waste.' She wanted to fulfil all her dreams in my marriage, as I was the first child of hers, and she also wanted to make my in- laws' family astonished by looking at what all mom had sent with me. She loved to get praises and she also wanted to get praised by my to-be in-law's families too. Therefore, she was putting her best.

One fine day, I started being presented to a bunch of families as a showpiece. The search was on, and simultaneously, I was made to have conversations with a few suitable proposals, and meanwhile, my parents narrowed it down to one to have a face-to-face meeting. I still remember the very first proposal meeting that came across to me. They were about to come see me at my house, and the house was being decorated as if it was some festival. Curtains and sofa covers were replaced. The dishes were arranged by top-branded sweet shops and restaurants. The platters were decorated with dry fruits, imported fruits, etc. The lunch was ordered from one of the best and costliest restaurants in my area. My parents, sister, and brother were running around, and I was instructed on how I needed to behave in front of the guests. My sister and mom took a short session with me, saying how I needed to behave, how much I needed to talk, what all I needed to do in front of them, blah blah blah, and so on. I know moms are the best, and they always think of their children and what is best for them. Being the obedient one, I grasped all the techniques and instructions from them. Meanwhile, my sister, sitting in front of the almirah, was also searching for the best dress and uttered in frustration, "Why have they decided to come on such short notice? I am not finding any perfect dresses for her in which she will look like a princess. If we had had time, we could have purchased some dresses for her from big brands."

My mom interrupted and calmed her, saying, "My *Rani* looks awesome in every dress. Choose any dress for her and she will enhance the beauty of the dress itself," and she kissed my forehead.

Finally, the moment arrived, and I was presented to them. My parents had a conversation with the guy. His parents talked to me about my interests, hobbies, job, etc. The whole scene was no less than a movie. Everything looked so dramatic. Both parties wanted to show their best to each other, and that was fun for me to observe.

There was a long chat going on between them, and the groom's party was entertained too much, and suddenly my mom said politely, "Come on, *Bhabhiji*, *Bhaisaab*, you guys are not having anything. Hey Raja, beta, you even have something. Try out these sweets; they are really delicious. We have specially ordered it and have requested the *mithai wala* to prepare it just for you all. We got this from one of the famous shops here. Even celebrities come to this shop to take this sweet home with them. Oh, please take these hot *paneer pakoras,*" and she instructed our servant to bring in more fresh, hot, grated *pakoras.*

The servant came and started serving it to everybody, and my mom instructed them, saying, "You go and manage the kitchen, I will serve them."

While serving them, my mom got emotional and uttered, "*Bhabhiji*, my *Rani* is very understanding, caring, and loving. She will shower love on all of you, which will always make you feel as if she is your own daughter. She will never let you do any work. My daughter is an expert at managing outdoors as well as indoors. I promise you that she will never let you all down. She will listen to everything, whatever you instruct her to."

And then she then silently signaled to me to serve the plates that she had prepared to serve everybody, and I went to help her with that.

Finally, after the long conversation and hearty laughs, our parents sent us to the foyer to talk to each other. I was excited as I liked everybody very much and was excited to start my journey with them. He was so caring, elegant, polite, and handsome. He was 6 feet tall with a well-built physique. The more I was with him, the more I started to develop a liking for him. Every girl has a fantasy about her would-be, and I would say he was something out of my dreams. He was an MBA graduate from one of India's top colleges and was earning not just 10 times, but 20 to 30 times more than what I was earning. My dream of living a king-sized life will be fulfilled if I marry him.

He did not ask me much. Looking at him, I understood that he is a reserved guy and talks selectively, but this was all that I always wanted in my spouse. We had a very brief chat as he did not ask me much, and when it was my turn, I did not prefer to ask him anything as I was feeling comfortable being with him. After a brief period, breaking the silence, he said, "Shall we move to our parents?" And I said yes, as I still was not getting words to speak at that moment, and we left. When we returned home, everybody looked at us expecting to know our decision, and suddenly his father asked him in his husky voice, "So how did you like her? Shall we move further with this proposal?"

At that moment, my heart started pounding as I liked the guy and was very afraid of his rejection. It was a happy and friendly family. One thing that I liked about them was the understanding that they had, which was easy to assess from their attitude. They were all so soft-spoken. The best thing which won my heart was that they were not greedy at all and had not demanded even a single penny as dowry. When my mom started telling them what all she had planned to gift me, they refused, saying that "we have everything and we don't expect *Rani* to get anything to our home. God has blessed us immensely, and we just want these two to be happy forever."

I was in my thoughts when suddenly I heard him say, "Yes." I was so elated. Suddenly everybody turned their eyes on me, expecting my reply, and I nodded yes too. After my affirmative response, there was a wave of happiness all around me. Afterward, we had lunch together, and a small *roka* ceremony happened where some amount of money was exchanged as *shagun*. This was the turning point in my life.

Soon we started dating each other. It was a very romantic and fantastic courtship period. We had a very brief period between our engagement and wedding, but we thoroughly enjoyed it. Every time I talked with him; I found a new trait in him. He was very witty, although he was close mouthed. I always wanted my life partner to be a clone of my father, and I was surprised to find him similar.

Believe me, you will experience the best lifetime experience during your courtship period. Those small outings, long drives, managing to sneak off from parents and meeting each other were truly an enriching experience and a lifetime treasure.

The best part of it was shopping. After all, which girl does not like to shop? Being in the spotlight and having everything around you gives you a unique feeling. The days went by quickly, and finally the D-day arrived.

IV

The wedding was done, and my parents presented it royally. Every guest was stunned by the amount of money that was spent by my parents. The decoration that was done was one of a kind. All the latest designs and decorations were selected by my parents. They did not leave any stone unturned, and everyone was found praising them. My parents gifted so much to my in-laws and *Raja*, although they denied accepting gifts and never asked for dowry. It was all my parents' wish and they were happy doing it all. After all, it was all about my father's reputation too. There is an old wives' saying, 'All's well that ends well', and we were so glad that it all went well. My parents gifted them with gold jewellery, costly brand dresses, and what not. They forced me to furnish my home with everything from a single needle to high-end furniture. I and *Raja* were made to reside in a house that was near to his office and was very far from his parents' place post marriage. Being able to manage everything all alone was a new and enriching experience. I decorated the house the way I always wanted to keep it. It was a unique feeling to stay with someone you don't know deeply for the rest of your life, leaving behind your parents. I communicated with my parents and siblings on a regular basis, as I was missing them badly. It is so painful for a girl to leave behind everything, be it her parents, loved ones, her own house, her bed, the place where she spent her childhood, her sister and brother, with whom she has a never-ending relationship. I don't know who has made the ancient custom where only a girl has to leave everything. With mixed emotions, I started sailing through the ocean of life. It was all going so smoothly and happily, making me feel like the luckiest woman in the world to have a husband like *Raja*. Yes, coincidentally, his name was *Raja* and mine was *Rani*. My mother also never got tired of praising *Raja* and my in-laws. But suddenly, after two months, things started to become weird. Slowly, I started feeling suffocated. I always heard that brightness is followed by darkness and vice versa, and something of a similar kind started happening to me. I was a working woman and was managing a house post marriage. Daily travelling to the office and coming back and managing things were getting worse day by day, and as on weekends, I wanted to stay back and relax at home, but my husband started forcing me to visit

his parents every weekend. Initially, it was all fine, but every weekend was getting hectic for me. He wanted to meet his parents badly, as he was the only son of his parents. He had a sister as well, but she was married and lived in another state. I never stopped him to meet them, but I wanted to have some rest, at least on weekends, so, once I collected courage, I tried to convey politely to him, "I am very tired *Raja*, as it has been the whole bunch of five days of me running from office to home and home to office. I need to take a rest as I am not well. Can we postpone the plan?"

And suddenly, I saw his expression getting upset, and he replied back to me, saying, "Ok. You take a rest; we will go next weekend to meet them. I will convey to them that you are not well and they will understand it too."

I felt relieved at that particular moment, but the similar acts continued thereafter. I even overheard my mother-in-law emotionally blackmailing *Raja*, saying, "It has been so long and you have stopped visiting us. We are desperate to meet and see you."

Why are in-laws always like this? Can't they focus their efforts on understanding a girl who is new to their family? Can't they learn to adjust with the new bride? Why are we expected to do everything, be it adjustments or just understanding them? When I, being a few months old, am expected to adjust to each and every one at their house, it isn't that easy for all of them to understand me, rather than forcing me alone to understand each and all in the family.

Somehow, the time went by with some happy moments and some days of blue. Happy was when I and *Raja* were together, living the best life and creating beautiful moments and wonderful memories to cherish my whole life. He was the one whom I loved at first sight. Every good thing is associated with a bad one, so I must discuss my blue moments too, it was when we were made emotional and blackmailed by my in laws to visit them regularly. It was a difficult task to manage along with managing my house and office, but somehow, we managed to contribute our time to them. I was always so good to them, but it started making me feel irritated when I was the only one who went there to meet them and do the household chores for them too. There was a double burden on me in those days. I used to get pissed off but never uttered a single word to them just because of my values and virtues. They, although being much older than my parents, had no concern for the girl who was managing her house along with the job and then managing their house too on most of the weekends. I must admit that girls have a pathetic life post-marriage. Before marriage, every girl is a princess to their parents, but after that, she is treated as a maidservant.

I still remember that once we all went out on a short trip with my in-laws, and while returning back, my mother-in-law got dangerously emotional. Sometimes I feel as if she is over dramatic and shows fake concerns just to engage my husband emotionally with her (Yes, he is my husband now, not just her son), but alas, here too, I am only expected to understand the situation where I can see my mother-in-law playing all kinds of tricks and tactics to pull my husband away from me to her. He 'was' her child, but now he 'is' my husband and I own equal rights on him. So, while we were leaving, she threw her prank and wanted to kiss on *Raja*'s forehead just to show her fake concerns, but *Raja* did not put his head down, so she kissed on his hand and then she turned to me. I got scared and showed my denial through my expression, but forcibly she still kissed me, pretending that she did not understand my expression or maybe she was trying to show her fake love towards me in front of her son to show how great and lovable she is to me. My mother never did this to us, and it all looked weird and awkward to me. You may believe it or not, but my mom-in-law is an overtly smart, adamant, old-rebellious woman with an orthodox mentality. My mom was right that in-laws could never ever be good. Anyhow, I was least concerned about my in laws but was more bothered about my husband.

Appropriately quoted by J. K. Rowling, 'Always the innocent are the first victims.' So, it has been for ages past, so it is now. And so, it was happening to me. I never uttered a single word in front of them, even though they were giving me all kinds of mental trauma. My in-laws were too smart in handling me. Although they never refused me anything, there was an implied no to everything I did. I started feeling suffocated when I was with them. I wanted to meet my parents because I had been missing them for about a month and it had been about a month since I had seen them; it all happened because my in-laws always asked us to come down to see them and my husband, an ardent devotee of his parents, would run to them. With time, he stopped caring about me. He would only listen to his parents' wishes and not mine. At least my mother-in-law should have thought about me. She must have gone through the same phase as I was going through.

At the dining table, while we were having dinner, she showed her fake concerns. To demonstrate her fraud care towards me in front of her son, she said, "Beta, go and visit your parents and siblings. They must be missing you a lot. " (And because of all this, my husband feels as if her mother cares a lot for me.)

And suddenly, *Raja* interrupted saying, "Mummy, she meets with her siblings very often. Did you forget that their college is nearby? So, they frequently pay her a visit.

Raja looked at me in a witty mood and said, "Right *Rani*?"

My mother-in-law suddenly said, "Then you can plan to visit and explore new places every weekend. You both will get ample time to spend with each other, and it will help you get to know and understand each other better. "

"Definitely, if you can spare us some 'we' time, but this is never going to happen because you are too obsessed with your boy," I said to myself.

Being innocent, I could not say anything except a 'yes'. *Raja* loved to meet his parents every weekend, but they wanted me to be happy with those short visits only. Was that justified? After all, I even wanted to be with my parents for a good number of days. After all, I had left everything to my husband, be it my place of birth, my toys, my bed, my friends, my relatives, my sister, my brother, my parents, and what would I expect in return from him? It was simply his concern and care for me. Anda little understanding would have done wonders for me. What else does a girl need from her husband?

Raja was a nice husband. He used to be the best when we were alone, and somehow was different when his parents were around. This behaviour used to irk me.

It seems today was the day when they all must have planned to speak about what irritates me the most. At the dinner table itself, while we were having our meal, my mom-in-law initiated again and looked at me and said, "So when are you getting us promoted?"

I got puzzled and reacted surprisingly, asking her what she meant to say.

She said it again. I must say, she shamelessly asked me about my plans to conceive a baby. I felt so shy. How could parents ask their kids about all this? It is my personal wish, and I never like anybody's interference in it. I never liked anybody forcing me to get into all this. I would not have liked it even if my mom had raised this question to me. It was hardly 6 months into my marriage and I had not enjoyed it yet. So much of fun was pending to be enjoyed, fulfilling my wishes for what I had dreamt of. It was my in-laws who were screwing up my life and not letting me have free time to enjoy, and now they wanted me to get trapped in all of those baby things.

She continued, "Look beta, now we both are getting older day by day and even want to have a glimpse of our grandchild, and you know that babies are the best reason for life. They make the whole environment light and happy."

Her words were making me lose my temper, but I did not say anything, as I do not have the habit of speaking out, so I just kept silent, thinking within, "If you both are getting old, that's not my problem. My mom is still so young. How could I make her *naani* at such a young age?"

V

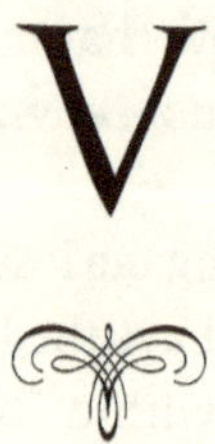

One fine morning, we were rushing to get to the office when the phone rang. I did not pick up the call as I was running to make everything quick as I was getting late for my office. The phone did not stop ringing. *Raja* hurriedly went to pick up the call. I could only hear *Raja* saying "Hello" and then I saw him fainting. I got scared and ran to him to hold him. When I reached for him, I could see tears in his eyes. He looked at me with his teary eyes and said, "Dad has got a paralytic attack."

We both ran to their place to check on his well-being. Luckily, he was out of danger. We stayed there for a long time, and the doctor instructed my husband, who is the only son of his parents, to take care of him and not to leave him alone ever again. My mom-in-law was all teary eyed. We consoled her, but she was overreacting. A person should be strong enough to face the entire situation, but my mother-in-law was just creating scenes. Later, I understood that this incident brought a horrendous tsunami into my life. My husband decided to travel a long distance to his office while staying at his parents' house and take care of him until he become perfectly fine. He even forced me to stay back with him at his parents' house to take care of them, but this was the biggest trauma. I somehow managed to stay back and take care of them for a couple of weeks, but soon it was hard for me to deal with them as my mom-in-law was too bossy while dealing with me as if I was some sort of maid. I never had the experience of being imprisoned at home. My father-in-law was improving day by day. So, I looked for an opportunity and discussed it with my husband, saying, "*Raja*, it has been so long since we have not gone to check our home. Now *papa* is also recovering well, so let's move back to our place. Mummy is smart enough to handle everything on her own. But *Raja*, in deep thought, nodded and said, "hmm..., but I think it's not the right time. Let him recover more and, although mummy is strong, she is too old to handle everything on her own." I felt frustrated. Hiding my emotions, I uttered, "But we have the responsibility of our home as well. I am getting worried; in what condition will our home be in now. We came here hastily and did not go there to check our home even once after that. I think we should go back." I don't know what I said, but *Raja*, for the first time, shouted at me, saying, "My father is more important to me than your house. Let that house go to hell. I can't leave my parents in this condition."

It was my first-time seeing *Raja* so furious, which made me scared and I got tears in my eyes. What did I say wrong? I did not ask him to leave his parents; rather, I was even taking good care of them, but *Raja* overlooked my efforts that I had put in to make his parents happy and regain their health. I had never worked this much in my life. If I had worked the same way at my mom's place, my mother should have appreciated me so much, but what did I gain here? I only reprimanded. I had never thought that my husband would ever shout at me. My father has never raised his voice against me till date, and *Raja* got the courage to insult me. I felt like running from there, so I went to *Raja* and told him, "I am leaving for my house now as I am worried about it. You stay back here." And then I started packing my bag. *Raja* did not bother to come and apologise to me, so I left, informing my mom-in-law andfather-in-law.

I bowed and touched their feet and said, "Mummyji, Papaji, some urgent work has come and I will have to leave. Please take care of yourselves."

VI

After leaving the place, I felt as if my wings got unclipped. It made me feel so light, and I decided to go to my parents' house instead of mine.

Finally, I could get the time and opportunity to go to my parents' house, which was, is, and will always remain mine. No place can replace my house, and its comfort can never be compared with anything existing in this world. The moment I stepped into my house, it made me feel very emotional, and I hugged my mom and started crying.

I was made to sit and relax while I was served my favourite dishes after a long time of making other people eat, cook, and serve by me at my in-law's house. I got tired of making other people eat, cook, and serve. After a long time, I was fed and I ate my mom's hand-cooked dishes. I was living every single moment with my family. It is always that you feel best with your loved ones and you always feel like a stranger in your in-laws' place. No matter how much you try to make them your own, they will not leave any stone unturned to make you realise that you are merely an outsider and stranger to them.

I was served a sumptuous meal, and after that, we all sat together to chit chat with each other. My siblings were pulling my leg, and my mom instructed them not to irritate me. This all brought tears into my eyes again. Looking at me teary-eyed, my sibling stopped playing around and became quiet. Looking at me getting emotional, my mom asked me, "What has happened beta? How is *Raja*? How is your father-in-law?"

Hearing *Raja*'s name, I burst out in tears.

My mom consoled me again, "Don't behave in such a way, darling; I may get panic attacks. At least say something. Is everyone alright? I had never seen my princess cry like this. What has made you cry? Who has made you cry? "

I got immense emotional support from my mom, which I had been craving for a long time. I said, "*Raja* shouted at me."

This made everybody surprised, and everyone asked me, in one voice, "But why?"

Listening to the whole narration of my story, my sister uttered, "This is so inhumane. How could anybody behave erratically? You did not say anything wrong. You just showed your concern to him about your house. I never thought that *Raja* would behave in such a way ever."

"And did he ignore all that you had done for his family? They made you work all day and night and did not realise your importance," said my mom, with tears in her eyes.

My brother was so furious that he was about to call *Raja* about his erratic behaviour, but I stopped him from doing so.

Now I was feeling much better as I shared my feelings inside and out with my loved ones.

Suddenly, my phone rang. I checked it; it was *Raja* calling. I did not feel like picking up the call from the one who had insulted me to the maximum extent. Hearing the long rings, my mom peeped into my phone, asking, "Hey, who is calling and why aren't you picking up the call?"

I murmured, saying, "It's *Raja*, and I am not willing to pick up his call."

But I had to receive his call at the insistence of my mother.

A calm voice came from him, asking, "*Rani*, didyou reach safely?"

I said "yes" in an indifferent tone.

Suddenly, my siblings entered my room shouting, which drew *Raja*'s attention, and he interrogated me, asking, "Where are you?"

And I casually replied, "At my home."

"What does my home mean?" *Raja* inquired. "I do have my own home too. I have my parents too. You are not only born to your parents or have parents. I do have them too. So, I'm at my mother's house," I responded erratically.

"But you did not inform me about it," uttered *Raja* again.

Hearing this, I got furious and replied back, saying, "I don't need anybody's permission to come to my place, my house. I have the full right to visit my house and my parents at any time I wish," and then disconnect the phone.

He is my husband, not my boss, from whom I need to get permission for whatever I do or wherever I go. I know it was not *Raja* who was speaking these sentences to me, but rather my mom-in-law must have fed all the ill-thoughts about me to him. She can never see me happy. My happiness was always troubling her. Are the girls bonded labour who need an authorization letter for whatever they do? I am a girl, but I am no less than a boy. I am equal to every boy. My gender doesn't allow me to get suppressed by the other existing genders in society. My life is my own, and I am the boss of my own life and nobody else's. I have not given anybody else the right to rule my soul. I am the queen of my own existence.

My anger had no boundaries and I was so furious that I decided to stay back with my parents till I felt comfortable being with them. After that, Raja also didn't bother to give me even a single courtesy call.

After a few weeks, I returned to my home, and I was surprised to find *Raja* there. It was the beginning of the next phase of our lives, which can be assumed to be the start of differences between us. The only question in my mind for *Raja* was: where did I go wrong? I cared for everybody in his family wholeheartedly, but still, I was never given respect by his family members, including him. Since I did not have any ego in me, I decided to initiate the conversation with *Raja*, as someone would have to take the initiative to start the conversation.

After this start by me, simultaneously over a period, everything became normal between us. We were once again the lovey dovey couple. One day, while I was in the arms of *Raja*, he put forth his wish to me, "*Rani*. I am planning to call Mummy and Papa to stay with us. You are aware that they are getting older and that they will require our assistance. You even take very good care of them and maintain a healthy bond with them. Mom even loves you very much and never gets tired of appreciating you. "

Trust me, I could feel how Nagasaki and Hiroshima could have felt after the atom bomb attacks, as his words were making me fume in my head.

Maybe he sensed my fury and further gave me the option, as if he was doing a favour to me and was so much concerned, "Whatever you wish, *Rani*. If you are not comfortable calling them here, we can shift with them. After all, we have a big house there and can live comfortably with our parents. And even your office is close by. Don't worry about me; I will manage somehow. "

There were thousands of things going on in my mind, but I kept quiet because of my moral rectitude. But the turmoil within me was not willing to stop. After all, I am a woman of the 21st century who prefers to live life on her own terms and conditions. I don't like being a burden on someone else and I don't like being burdened by someone. How will I reach the pinnacle of my life if I am always entangled in legal relations? I realised with my experience of about 8 to 9 months since marriage that staying with mom-in-law would ruin my professional as well as personal life if I agree to stay with them as she is imperious. I was told before marriage that I would be living at a distant place from my in-laws, and it was also one of the many reasons for me to pursue this proposal. The dilemma before me was how to say no to my husband. I tried to think hard, but I ended up being good as I am by nature and said, "OK" and agreed like an obedient wife.

My affirmative response made *Raja* so happy that he hugged me tightly and kissed me. I realised that day that I, and my happiness, meant nothing to him. It was only about him, himself, his parents, and his family where I could not findmyself anywhere.

VII

The night went into turmoil in my brain, and I had difficulty sleeping. Somehow, I got drowsy, but I felt uncomfortable and felt discomfort in my tummy. I ran to the washroom and puked everything out. I felt so weak and sat in the bathroom itself to gather some energy to get to my bed, but I could not. Meanwhile, *Raja* arrived, searching for me because I was missing in bed, and assisted me in reaching my bed. I had almost run 6 to 7 times and had no energy left to get up and prepare breakfast.

Raja was there beside me, caring for me and looking at the clock for the hospital to start OPD.

We got ready, and I did not know that this day had another bombing plan for me. The doctor checked me properly and happily congratulated us, saying to *Raja*, "Congratulations, your wife is pregnant."

It was a bolt out of the blue for me, but *Raja* became so happy knowing this. This news shook me. I got chills going down my spine as I wasn't ready for this. I could not accept it as so many of my wishes were still unfulfilled. I could not show any trace of happiness on my face.

Raja happily said to me, "Wow, I am so happy, *Rani*. Thank you for all this. I am the luckiest husband. I know that Mummy and Papa will be elated to know this. They had been waiting for this day for a long time."

We returned from the hospital, but somewhere inside me, I wasn't ready for all this. I was so upset that I couldn't accept the truth, and thousands of ideas raced through my mind about how to abort the baby and avoid being blamed by *Raja* and his family. Couple of months ago, a similar incident happened, but I managed to abort the baby without passing this piece of information to anyone, but this time I wasn't sure about my pregnancy and *Raja* got to know before me, making the task of abortion difficult for me. A girl doesn't have any right to her wish. I was not at all ready for it. Tears were just rolling down my cheeks as this news was not what I always wanted. I was about to lose my independence with all this. Your mind should be prepared to accept the physical and mental changes that come with conceiving a child. All surrounded by divergent thoughts, I was silent on the way home.

As soon as I arrived, I requested *Raja* not to disturb me as I was not feeling well and locked up myself in a room and called my guiding light-'my mom.' Mom's voice has a special quality as it soothes your pain. Since our inception into the world, the very first sound that we hear since our antenatal days inside mom's womb is our mamma's voice. For every kid, it is most melodious sound than any other sound existing in the world. And my thoughts were interrupted by her question, "What happened, dear? Why aren't you speaking? Do you have any worries?"

Moms are the best creations in the world because they can read a child's brain at any time and every time with 100% precision.

I responded by saying "Yes" in a very low voice.

The compassion in her voice made me open my heart out to her, and I started crying and expressing myself to her, saying, "Mummy, I am pregnant!"

There was a happy tone, and she interrupted, saying, "That's good news, darling." Congratulations. You don't worry at all. "Your Mummy is there and she will take care of everything. "

I interrupted her and said, "But Mommy, I am not ready for it at all as I haven't ticked all the boxes on my wish list yet." I haven't found time for myself and have just become like a rolling stone. I'm just moving to and fro from my place to the in laws'. What about me, my life, my wishes, my happiness?"

After listening to me, my mom said to me, "You need to put up a brave front, darling." Life post-marriage is a tight rope walk. It's all a part of life, and you are the one who needs to balance everything. Just sit back, relax, and think. You will find an answer to every question. And if you trust me and my words, believe me, you should have this baby as the baby strengthens the bond between spouses. They act as a nuclear force that is difficult to break, and as you mentioned earlier, this baby will focus his entire attention on you. He will not find time to think about anyone except his baby and you. He won't think about his own parents either. "

Mummy's words made me recollect the moment when *Raja* became very happy after hearing this news. I had never seen him so excited and cheerful till date and I interrupted Mummy, saying, "Yes, Mummy, he was very excited about hearing this."

The conversation with Mummy made me feel very relaxed, and I was feeling better than before, as all I wanted was attention and love from *Raja*, which I could gain through our baby. I decided to pull it off myself, so I opened the door with a cheerful smile and went and sat next to *Raja*.

Raja, with a concerned expression, asked me about my well-being, and his every action had already started making me feel special as he was just thinking of me and was concerned about me. I wish that now the rest of my life would be as per my wish.

Raja told me with glee that his mother and father are overjoyed and have thanked you for honouring their wish. You will be happy to know that mom and dad will be joining us soon to take care of you since you will require more time to rest, a balanced and healthy diet to eat, and a motherly touch of care.

VIII

The very next day, I got up late as I could not sleep the previous night and wasn't feeling well. I could hear someone talking outside in the living room, so I opened it to check and was shocked to see that my in-laws were there. I got ready and stepped out of my room and touched their feet. My mother-in-law kissed my forehead, which always irritated me the most, but I did not react. They came with their huge luggage, as if they had planned to settle with us. Not able to resist myself, I popped the question to them: "How did you manage to reach here?"

To which *Raja* replied, "I went to pick them up. How was it possible for mom and dad to reach here on their own? I did not disturb you as you were in deep sleep and could not sleep the previous night as well as the whole day."

Although I was frustrated, irritated, and what not, sometimes you are left with no option except to accept the present situation, so I planned to sail through the wave. From day one, the dictatorship of my mom-in-law started. She started enforcing her orders on me, even though I was a grown-up woman to understand what was better for me or the baby inside me. Initially, I did not say anything, but soon the words started to get on the tip of my tongue, but again, recollecting the lessons of values taught by my parents, I swallowed everything.

My mom-in-law used to get behind me, forcing me to drink milk, which I have hated the most since childhood, and then forcefully make me eat a big bowl full of fruit, which irked my gastro - intestinal tract. Making me eat non-oily patient-like food for so many days was making me sicker and more upset. Soon, I started getting cravings for pizza, burgers, French fries, ice creams and a lot more. I was sick and tired of being fed home-cooked food and her restrictions on me on whatever I wished to eat. My mom-in-law always used to pester me, saying, "Beta, you should quit consuming junk foods as it is not good for the baby's health. In our days, we never ate things that harmed babies. It's our responsibility to think of our baby before us. We are the ones to take care of our baby. "

Her never-ending storytelling and long instructions were getting difficult to bear day by day and was getting on my nerves. I desperately wanted to have some 'me time' as she was always around me, 24x7 caressing me, sitting beside me on my bed when I desperately needed to be alone. Everything within a certain limit looks good, and beyond that, it starts making you feel that you are being interfered with.

The mood swings were on high and I was not the same as I was before. I was surrounded by strangers with whom I had not even stayed together for even a year, which was not making me comfortable. Still, I was trying to be my best at a time when every girl wishes to be surrounded by loved ones who understand her inside and out perfectly.

My mother-in-law began spoon-feeding my husband and teaching him to meddle in my life in the name of concern and care, possibly because she was dissatisfied with her interference in my life. This routine and new normal was getting abnormal for me. Persistent intrusion by both of them irritated me the most, and since I could not say anything to my in-laws, I started having frequent arguments and fights with *Raja*. It is difficult to survive in a traumatic situation, upon sensing that my in-laws were encroaching in my life, I hid my irritation and went to her and politely conveyed, "Mummy ji, I know that you care a lot for me, but too much of interference is getting on my nerves now. Still, I have my mom to think or decide what is good for me and to guide me, even she is a mother of three, so with folded hands, I would appreciate if you spare me alone with no interference anymore. It will be better if you head towards your house and let me live peacefully at my house". I said this with no intention of hurting anyone, but only to prevent myself from stepping into hell. I stood for myself, as I was always taught that I would have to stand for myself; nobody else would come to take a stand for me.

I always tried to express myself to them since I wanted them to understand me well as I was the new addition to the family and they must not be well aware of my habits and behaviour. Since childhood, I was a very silent girl who loved to have her privacy, so wanting not to create any misunderstanding between me and my extended family, I exercised my mind enough to go and admit my present mental situation to them.

But it seems it was not well absorbed by my in-laws, as they left my place the very next day. Since the day my in-laws left, my husband has stopped interacting with me and has started to behave arrogantly. Every pregnant lady needs care, love, and support from her spouse. But mine was different, and even my in-laws took me wrong and left me alone in this condition when a pregnant woman needs the utmost care. It seemed no one in the house was ready to accept me and understand me. It hurts when everybody makes a gang against you in the house. There is a wise old man saying that 'Innocence is a kind of insanity,' and so I was, a bit insane to consider my husband my partner in every thick and thin. Maybe I was bearing the brunt, as I was of the type who used to call a spade a spade, very truthful and frank. I soon realised that my husband was a chip off the old block. Every parent should teach their son to be compassionate with patience towards his wife, but in the era of patriarchy, it's hard to find. Only we women are wrong, and never ever the masculine community, 'the man.'

Because I was feeling trapped by the circumstances, I decided to call my mother to look after me when everyone else left me alone. My parents arrived; I hugged my mom and I got head over heels to see them. I expressed what I was going through to my parents, assuming that *Raja* was not at home, but suddenly *Raja* entered the house as he came early and heard our conversation without my knowledge. Now, he has started spying on me too. I have the right to discuss my part with my parents. Suddenly, *Raja* went to my mom and complained to her about my behaviour towards his parents and pointed a finger at the morality with which my upbringing was done. I must admit, he was very rude in his expression. He was playing the devil's advocate. Seeing all this happening, I lost my head. Seeing me living in a hell-like situation, my mom instructed me to pack my bags, so I packed everything I needed, and left home, filled with rage at the insult that was done to my mom by him. I wasn't born to be the target of my mother's snub. Every girl can withstand an insult or torture, but she will never see her parents getting insulted. While I was leaving, I was expecting him to realise his mistake and say sorry to my parents, but he did not bother to stop me nor even he said sorry to my parents. On realising that I held no importance or position in his life, I decided to leave the place with the ones for whom I was a priority and who could never see me in pain since my childhood.

IX

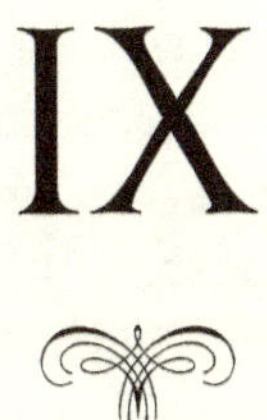

Days went by and I was in the best of hands for care. My mum used to take care of my daily needs. Starting right from the early morning, she made me drink milk, fruits, healthy home-cooked food and what not. Rather than just saying no to fast food, she made me understand why pregnant women should never eat junk food. There should always be a way to make other people understand rather than just being bossy like my mom-in-law used to be. No one in the world can take care of you as your mother can. The days passed by like this, and *Raja* never turned up. I always had my eyes and ears on the phone, expecting his call, but it never happened. I was carrying a chip on my shoulder because the reason for the dispute was serious, and I never called him up because he made a mistake and I wanted him to realize his mistake and apologise for it. Month by month, time flew away until my delivery day finally arrived. I had a sudden pain, and I was rushed to the hospital for delivery. I was in unbearable pain and was taken to the delivery room immediately.

Doctors and staff gathered quickly as the baby's heart rate was slowing down. They decided to further monitor, and after an hour, they decided to operate as soon as possible as the baby's condition was worsening.

It took almost an hour and the c-sec was done. I was blessed with the beautiful princess, my baby girl. Everybody was happy, and my eyes were searching for something to see, and my ears were eager to hear about *Raja*, but surprisingly, they did not show up in the hospital. I asked my parents whether they had informed them, and they nodded, saying 'Yes.' It made me feel very upset.

After a few days, at the insistence of my family, they turned up, but they did not stay back at our place for long. They just had a glimpse of the baby with a frown on their face and then left, never to return. I surrendered my situation to my faith and slowly started adjusting to the situation that was presented to me by my fate.

Days went by, slowly turning into weeks, months, and then years. The reason for my life at the moment was just one thing, and that was my little daughter. Now I could realise the importance of having my child, which I was never in favour of. I could slowly understand the reason for my in-laws and husband not turning up; it was just because I gave birth to a 'girl'. If it had been a boy, they all probably would have accepted me and the baby wholeheartedly. Still, she was my daughter, and I could not dump her anywhere. My life started circumambulating around her. Although I still had intense support from my family, I wanted my husband to come and accept his fault, and only then did I have plans to accept him and move with him. But since I gave birth to a girl, they had plans to dump me and my girl. As in today's era, girls are considered mere responsibility, a burden, and nothing more than that. But, as a mother, I promised myself that I would give my daughter the best life possible; one in which she would never have to compromise on anything, and in which she would be able to fight for anything for herself.

After many years, I started to realise that *Raja* was never going to come back, and as drastic times call for drastic measures, I decided to take a few extreme steps to make them realise the mistake that they had committed. It was never my loss; rather, it was theirs, as they were not blessed to record all the unforgettable innocent acts of their little munchkin. How could a father be so ruthless as to not turn up for his child's and disown her? But I, being a mother, can never leave my child or make him live a life with low confidence. As I was being presented with the circumstances, slowly I started to give up my emotions, which were attached to *Raja*. I was helpless and shattered to take this step, but had no other options left. I was his with all of my heart and soul, but he was unconcerned about me and made no effort to become mine. As he never bothered for me, bothered me more with each passing day. My life was becoming hell with each day. Looking at my condition and sympathising with me, I was being suggested by my friends, aunties, relatives, and colleagues to take legal action on the extended family. Initially, I felt that this was all mumbo jumbo by them, but once my mom's friend visited and said, "Oh, I feel pity looking at her. How cheerful she was. Look at her, how she has become now." That incident shook my soul.

Sometimes it made me feel that I had become a joke to them. And *Raja* was the one responsible for everything that happened to me or in whatever condition I was in. He has crossed the line in everything.

After the brief period of me being in trauma, I realised that I am still self-dependent as I always was, and hence I decided to take stringent legal action against them for spoiling my life. My soul would get peace only if I could see their lives becoming hell. The time has come for me to either succeed or fail. My journey was surely in tatters. My ego was no less than another guy's ego. Why is it that women are born slaves while all men are born free? Why should I be going through this phase all alone? I should drag them to court and make their lives worse than mine. There is a well spoken wise man's saying, "We've let the blade of our innocence dull over time," and even Tiffany Madison quoted it so appropriately, "No one loses their innocence." It is either taken or willingly given away, as has happened to me. I am an educated girl of the modern era, knowing all the rights and provisions provided to me by Indian law. I rolled up my sleeves to take revenge for every bit of pain I had suffered due to my husband and in-laws. My sufferings were unforgettable, so I wanted to make their sufferings haunting for them too. I held my daughter in one hand and the feminist laws in the other, making me the most powerful. The time has arrived to become happy by seeing them suffering by each passing day. My peace was now directly proportional to their sufferings.

X

"When life presents you with a lemon, lemonade doesn't remain the only option. It can make your life sour too."

My train arrived at the station, and I boarded it. It was difficult to search for my name on the reservation chart, which was pasted on the train, as everyone was gathered at the entrance gate of the train, making it difficult for me to enter. But somehow, I managed to have a glance out of the crowd and check my berth number on the reservation chart: Name-*Raja*, Berth Number-26. Seeing your name on the reservation chart gives you a feeling similar to that of checking the result of the engineering entrance test and finding your name there. It was packed with passengers, a few standing in front of the washroom requesting T.T. to provide them with a berth. Looking at them, I considered myself lucky, in this context at least, when luck was busy playing hide and seek with me. It happened many times when I travelled a long distance sitting in front of the bathroom. I was dead tired the whole day since the week was very hectic. I had lots of pending work in the office, and I needed to travel a long distance, covering almost 3200 km for3 days via train.

I sat on my seat and looked around to have a look at my co-passengers, and suddenly a girl sitting next to me greeted me, cheerfully, saying, "Hi."

I greeted her back. It was a dark night outside, and although I was dead tired, I wasn't feeling sleepy at all and was restless the whole night. When I turned towards my front berth, I found the same girl who greeted me. She was wide awake and smiled at me. She wanted to start a conversation as it was a long journey and we were both not feeling sleepy. She said, "Aren't you feeling sleepy?"

I replied, "No."

Then she said, "But you look very tired." I nodded my head in affirmation.

She continued, "So where have you been? Do you stay here or have you just come as a tourist to visit this place?"

I said, "No, I came here fora purpose."

She was in no mood to stop her questionnaire and seemed to be very excited, she asked, "For what? What could it be other than exploring the place or visiting the hometown? "

I replied blatantly, "I came here to attend a court hearing."

She jumped to a conclusion and said, "So you are a lawyer."

I said, "No, I am not."

"Oh! Then are you a murderer?", she asked me jokingly.

I replied her saying, "I have a criminal case going on in my name."

Her expressions changed, but she did not stop questioning and continued, "Oh, so you are a criminal."

After a brief pause, she continued, "Don't mind, but you look so calm, naive, compassionate, and from a good family. How could you get into legal trouble? Did you kill anyone or have you robbed someone?", She asked me in a low but curious tone.

"No, it's a divorce and matrimonial case," I spoke.

Looking at her inquisitive mind, I also decided to talk to her and open my heart to her, despite the fact that it had been years since I had kept everything within me, which was slowly eating me up day by day, like what a termite does to a solid wood, no matter how hard and of the highest quality it is. And thus, I started narrating my story to her and asked her, "Are you married?"

She replied excitedly, "No, but I'm getting married soon. Actually, I had gone to meet my fiancé. I am so excited. Isn't it fun to marry? He is the best, exactly as I had always dreamt of. He is the same as I always wanted my 'would be' to be, so caring and loving. Not just him, his family members are too good and have promised to keep me happy just like their daughter. "

Suddenly, her words took me back to my initial days when my wife told me how she felt about me when I met her for the first time. It was all very similar. Does every girl feel the same?

I interrupted her, saying, "And what have you promised to them?"

She fumbled, "Promised? I mean, what promise? Why will I promise them? After all, it's me who is leaving her house and everything, so it is their responsibility to keep me happy, not mine to keep them happy. "

Hearing her, I satirically smiled, and observing my expressions, she got a bit annoyed and asked me, a bit arrogantly, about the reason for my satirical smile. I answered her query, "Marriage is not just fun, but it is also a responsibility. Even in a bed of roses, you may encounter thorns too that may hurt your finger or a tiny body part. That doesn't mean that you discard that body part completely. Marriage is something in which you both need to contribute 100% of each other's part; it is only in divorce that you divide everything in half. It is not necessary for one of the spouses to shoulder all of the responsibility through thick and thin; rather, both should work on it. Marriage is about sharing, whereas divorce is all about tearing. It is a delicate thread initially, but as it grows year after year, the trust, which is built over time, the love, care, concern, and many more keep depositing on the thread making it thick like a rope almost impossible to break due to delicate reasons. You will be surprised to know that marriage, being a single word in itself, contains the faith of the whole universe. It may add stars to somebody's life, or it may sometimes hit so hard that you start seeing stars in the daylight. Since you are going to start marital life in a few months, I, being a senior and experienced, must share some know-how about marriage with you.

There are five stages in total: The first one is the LOVEY-DOVEY STAGE, which I must say you are enjoying currently. In this, you are in awe of your partner, and each other's company falls short of the time. 24 hours seems like less in a day. You will be each other's apples of the eye, with your eye in his eye. In short, I must say that you will fall head over heels in love with each other. This one is the best of all the other stages. From being "you are my only," there is a shift to the next stage, which is the "RUDE AWAKENING STAGE." I must describe this stage as the surprising and unpleasant discovery that one is mistaken, or I could call it the 'earth-shattering awakening.' Here you start playing the game of 'finding flaws' and the curtain starts rising from each other's behaviour, which they 'pretended to be' in the early stages. 24 hours in a day will seem enough to you at this stage, and a dilemma continues between you having a few romantic days and nights and having a few nights and days frustrated due to some or other abnormal and irritating behaviour of your partner noted by you. If you manage to go through this up and down and adjust yourself to this bitter truth of reality, you will succeed in pulling off your marriage to the third stage, which is the "TUG OF WAR STAGE". Congratulations to you, as you are successful in getting yourself into an anguish phase, or rather, it would be better to define it as an affliction, or I could say a discomfort phase. Withstanding your spouse for 24 hours slowly becomes a big question for you, and I would preferably say that this profile generally shows an increasing trend that is an increase in suffocation kind of feeling with time, so either of you would start pulling away from each other and would rather spend less time with each other. Rather than clarifying the issues, you would prefer to complain about each other to your parents, siblings, or friends, and if you are lucky, they, being your close ones, will understand your emotions and provide you with strong support as well as a number of instructions on how to deal with your spouse. This will act as if you were adding pure *desi ghee* to the spark that was generated between you two. Some of you could sense the brewing up of differences within you and would opt for a path to resolve this trouble, but some prefer to retain their ego and continue to humiliate each other, and soon the thought of leaving each other starts occupying the brain. You're both losers when it comes to working as a team, and you're on your way to breaking up because you see each other as the source of your pathetic life. Most divorces happen at this stage. "

Suddenly, I got interrupted by *Jaya*, saying in a stressed tone, "You ended my marriage before it even started."

I laughed and said, "Don't lose patience and listen as there are still two stages left. You must have heard that every storm is followed by a silent one. The next, I mean, the fourth stage, is the "STAGE OF BALANCING/JUGGLING ACT," where you start gaining confidence that although your partner is not perfect, he is manageable and you could survive being with him, and soon you start liking him or her for what they are in the original, considering their flaws becomes the strength of this relationship. You will be eager to resolve your issues, concerns, and dislikes with each other. At this stage, 24 hours will still be enough for you to spend with your partner. Although it is difficult to reach this stage, some do so with flying colours and succeed in saving their marriage. After all these stages, the last and the fifth one come as "HAPPILY EVER AFTER STAGE," as it is quoted at the end of the movies. It is a vicious circle that is followed; hence it again connects you to the Lovey Dovey stage, but surprisingly, according to the Relationship Institute, less than 5% of couples reach to this stage. Again, 24 hours will be less for you in a day for you to be together. By the time you reach this stage, you start considering yourself and your partner as "one soul and two bodies" and have succeeded in your team effort. If, initially, you were feeling content by bitching about your partner, reaching this stage will make you furious if you find someone even raising their voice at him/her. Your bond will be considered as an example to illustrate to newlyweds, and your marriage will be considered a kind of fairy tale in which we find two souls truly in love dedicated to each other.

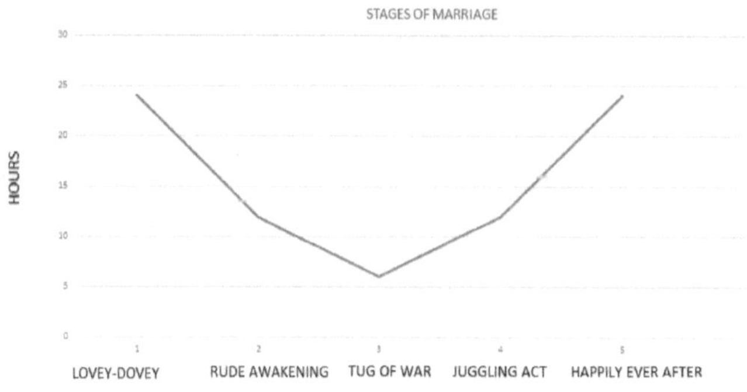

As I finished, she jumped in between and said, "You have good knowledge about marriage and relationships. So why did you fail in your relationship?"

I laughed at myself and resumed imparting knowledge, "Marriage is all about balance between the two souls who have different upbringings, values, and virtues. Rather than putting ourselves in each other's shoes, we prefer to throw shoes at each other. Every individual has their own strong egos, and ultimately, it ends up becoming a fight of egos more than a fight between husband and wife. The husband stops considering her as a wife and wife stops considering the man as her husband. Slowly, the pious bond becomes a poisonous bond."

XI

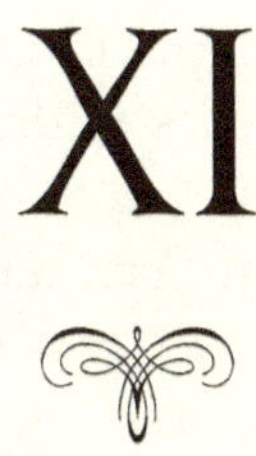

Suddenly, the feminism hidden in her spoke out: "Definitely, the husband should start treating and respecting the wife well. Which girl would prefer to have a break-up? Men usually torture women so much that they are helpless to take such steps. I had read in the news that during the lockdown period of the Corona pandemic, there was a surge in domestic violence cases. Men are always at fault, and women can never be."

I took a deep breath and said, "It is the irony of today's world that women are always right and no men are left to be considered right. Oscar Wilde, the Irish poet, put it very well: "I think God, in creating man, somewhat overestimated his ability." There are so many stereotypical thoughts regarding men, and it's very hard to eradicate them from the minds of individuals. It is so ingrained genetically that it will be passed down to future generations, and no one would make an effort to look into men's hearts and emotions. I somehow feel so unlucky to be born as a man. We can't express emotions, as some statements imply that men cannot feel hurt. We have the same sensory receptors, the same nerve fibres, the same spinal cord, and the same brain stem through which the pain travels as that of a female. So, if girls are permitted to shed their tears, why can't boys? Why, since childhood, are boys taught that boys, or I can say, real men, don't cry? I always recollect the lyrics of the rock band 'The Cure,' which says,

"I try to laugh *about it. Cover it all up with lies. I tried to laugh about it.*

Hiding the tears in my eyes

'Cause boys don't cry Boys don't cry. "

I remember I was hardly six years old and was asked by my uncle to go and purchase coriander leaves worth five rupees from a kiosk in front of our house. It was the first time I was sent alone, as I was a grown-up child in my elder's view, since I was the eldest among the kids in the family and because I was a 'boy'. I was scared to step out of my house initially, but still gathered the courage to do so. I was happy while returning as I did it by myself for the first time, but when I handed it over to my uncle, he scolded me as the shopkeeper cheated on me. I was reproached badly and was told that I didn't have maturity and a brain and that I was not smart enough to carry responsibilities. That incident, although a small one, still has an immense impact on my brain. Is a six-year-old mature enough to be given responsibilities and, rather than appreciating them, does he deserve a scolding? I did not cry that day, although I was very upset. I did not even express this to my mom because indirectly I was taught that 'boys don't cry'. I remember the beautiful lyrics of the Sparks band, which are assimilated in me, showing boys are waterproof:

"*The rain just falls off of me The tears just fall off of me*
'Cause I'm waterproof, I'm waterproof
The barometric pressure has no relevance to me."

This extremely venomous society has a belief that emotionally expressive males are 'weak' or are judged as 'gay.' But now I realise that maybe my uncle, my family members were preparing me to face the worst that was yet to come in my life. No matter how hard you work, you will always be regarded as a second-class citizen and will always be looked at as having been downgraded.

Do you know that 'sexual dimorphism' is the scientific term for physical differences between males and females of a species? But we are no different than girls biologically, and we originate from the same mass of embryonic tissue. If someone thrashes us, pricks us, slaps us, or commits any other form of physical violence against us, we experience the same level of pain as a female would. We are not born with bullet proof jackets rather we are forced to put on unreal unexpressive jacket which instructs our mind to become unresponsive to our own emotion. Being a boy is no longer a boon to us; rather, it has become a bane. Due to the stereotypes or preconceived ideas about the roles, abilities, and characteristics of males and females, which contain significant distortions and inaccuracies, we are stamped by the word 'masculinity' and, surprisingly, this word is eating us up from the inside. If we comply with this word, we will be blamed; if we don't, or say, deviate from or violate gender role norms of masculinity, we will still be blamed; some will even call us impotent. If someone puts effort into going deep into this regressive ideology of 'traditional masculinity', they will find that it has put a limit on men's psychological development, hence negatively influencing their mental and physical health. Men are four times more likely to die of suicide than women worldwide.

The term 'patriarchy' is heavily vilified and is used as a weapon against men by feminists, but this so-called patriarchal society is also an enemy to men, putting enormous pressure on men to keep things under control by detaching our tongues and rendering us speechless, rather than confining us to the closed chamber of our own minds and rendering us dumb. We are enslaved by the stereotypical sayings and gender discrimination that were instituted by early society and are still being continued. Is that me who has asked society to keep their thoughts male-biased? I don't know why men don't raise their voices against the patriarchy. Because we have a tag of being male, the expectations of everybody else have no limits for us. Because of these patriarchal thoughts, our lives have become hell. When we grow up, we are made to understand our role and duties towards our family and are pressured to excel in studies to have a stable career, as we are boys, to accomplish our lives so that we can create shelter for everybody to live in and arrange sumptuous food for everybody in the family on the table. We have always worked hard for the family, whether it is parents or wife and children, but it all goes to waste when your hard work is taken for granted and there are no words of appreciation. When men gather the courage to express themselves, which is well understood by a mother, but rarely understood by a wife. Those husbands whose wives understand them are lucky, but I wasn't lucky enough to have a happy married life. My mom never stopped me from fulfilling my responsibilities towards my wife, but it was always misunderstood by my wife, and I was stopped from doing my duties towards my parents. I was the one who had to listen to both the parties and absorb everything within me like a sponge without showing any sign of reaction. But surprisingly, my deadpan expression was still a problem for my wife, and she used to start fights with me by deviating from the topic of my *maa*. I thought that I was being smart enough by staying neutral towards both, but I forgot that wives are far cleverer than we can imagine.

Well, the relationship between mother-in law and daughter-in-law is like Tom and Jerry, who can't withstand each other and would not even ignore each other without any unnecessary indulgence in each other's territory just to lead a peaceful life. The irony is also that when we find a good mother-in-law, our daughter-in-law will not be good and vice versa, and surprisingly, they both consider themselves the best. Girls have a typical mentality of never being satisfied with anything they get; they don't value what God has gifted them with; rather, they always carry a feeling that 'the grass is always greener on the other side'. And the best happens with the husband, who is like a prophet who is not honoured in his own country. Despite the fact that I lived far away from my elderly parents, my wife always had problems with them and would always complain about them to me. I have grown up with the lessons of fulfilling my duties and respecting every relationship, and I still feel that it's easy to break, but it takes immense effort to keep anything intact. After all, we are social animals and will have to survive with other people surrounding us. How can I turn my back on my parents and sister? Once, I tried to make my wife understand, but she got furious and did not speak to me for almost a month. Now, I have become a strong believer that women are God's most complex creation. I am perplexed by what they demand. If we listen to their wishes, they will have a feeling that we are not smart enough to take any decision or take any stand. If we ignore their wishes and don't listen to them, they will start crying, cursing, and, surprisingly, the intensity of their anger keeps on increasing at a very high pace, which usually ends with threats.

Trust me, men are simple souls, and we want our lives to be simple too. But women waste their whole day, week, month, or year just analysing men and end up making everything complex."

After bearing me for so long, womanism in her resurfaced with a vengeance. Although girls are impatient and can hardly let the boys speak, it seemed it was my day and I was in no mood to leave this opportunity to express what a man is to a woman, educating her enough not to spoil any man's life further. She interrupted me, "Yes, we girls do have immense emotions in us, and this makes our hearts pure. We speak as we feel, but that doesn't mean that we are complex creatures. There are and will always be differences between men and women, and they cannot be the same species."

She said enough for me to jump to continue to demonstrate and to show her the real picture by busting the myth, and I again started, "Miss, I would like to draw your attention to the fact that although men and women don't always see eye to eye, biologically, they are a lot more similar than most of us realize. You must be astonished to know that we both have the same hormones; there is nothing like 'male' and 'female' hormones. The difference between the two is only in the levels, patterns, and how the hormones interact with male and female bodies. In men, testosterone is produced mainly in the testes, whereas in women it is produced in the ovaries, adrenal glands, fat cells, and skin cells. Combined with estrogen, testosterone helps with the growth, maintenance, and repair of a woman's reproductive tissues, bone mass, and human behaviour. Similarly, a particular form of estrogen known as estradiol in males is crucial for male sexuality; it modulates libido, erectile dysfunction, and spermatogenesis, and even men rely on progesterone to preserve their masculinity. In fact, progesterone is a precursor to testosterone. One more fact which I would like to share with you is that the brains of men and women are the same, with no reliable and repeatedly demonstrated morphological brain differences, except a slight size difference among them. It has been observed that behavioural differences like physical aggression and aspects of reproduction have a direct bearing due to the biological dissimilarity between males and females, whereas research has shown that there is much more biological similarity (like in the brain) between males and females than differences. So why do we almost always try to explain behaviour by implicating biological (evolutionary) differences between the sexes? Isn't it possible for women to be aggressive like men, or for men to be naive, understanding, and helpful, with all of the societal characteristics that only a woman can provide as per society? If biological differences were the sole reason, then why do women show aggression and commit crimes that are equally heinous as men? Why do they cook up false stories just to satisfy their ego and to sense the feeling of victory by harassing their in-laws' family and husband? There was a saying that a woman makes up the family, but she is the one who just doesn't destroy; rather, she roots out the family and snatch away all the happiness of the men and their near and dear ones too. They are clever enough to grab all the opportunities to pester the opposite sex just to gain mental and emotional satisfaction." Suddenly, I was distracted by the nostalgic voice of tea-seller "Chai-Chai" inside the compartment. I could not resist myself from taking a sip of the tea.

XII

After finishing tea, I continued, "The women are loaded with *amour propre* about themselves for being what they are born as, severely obsessed with themselves and in self-love, and definitely why not behave the same when they are lucky enough to be gifted by chiliad sections in law supporting them blindfolded, whereas we are punished fora crime that is not even committed by us, just because we are men and we are assumed to be 'masculine'. There are not just legal but also constitutional provisions for women in India. You name it, they have it just to screw up your life. Usually, constitutional rights are for the needy; they try to do justice to each stratum of society, but surprisingly, the result is always in favour of women and never for men.

The constitutional privileges gifted to women are: Article 14, i.e., equality before the law for women; prohibits the state from discriminating against any citizen solely on the basis of religion, race, caste, sex, place of birth, or any combination of these factors; the state must make special provisions for women and children; the State shall direct its policy toward securing for men and women equally the right to an adequate means of livelihood; equal pay for equal work; equal opportunity; and to provide free legal aid by suitable legislation to ensure justice is not denied because of economic or other disabilities; the State shall make provision for just and humane working conditions and maternity relief; the State shall promote educational and economic interests in order to protect them from discrimination; the State shall promote educational and economic interests in order to protect them from discrimination;

Allow me to take you on a brief tour of the legal provisions that are in place.

IPC 376, IPC Sec. 302/304-B, IPC Sec. 498- A, IPC Sec. 354, IPC Sec. 509

And suddenly she interrupted, perplexed, saying, "What are these numbers all about?"

I replied, in a witty sense, "Soon you will get to know what these numbers are all about. I used to wonder a few years back about the use of the numbers which we were taught in mathematics during our school days and soon realised maybe our school was preparing us for this day."

Not understanding my jest, she asked me again, "I did not get you. Can you please elaborate on what you said?"

I don't know whether she asked me to explain the above with feminist curiosity or meninists, but still, I explained it to her, hoping that maybe the conveying of information from me to her may save at least one Indian family, and I continued, "You are privileged by law and are protected against crimes under Indian Penal Codes (IPCs) of: Rape, Homicide for Dowry, Dowry Deaths or their attempts, Torture, both mental and physical, Molestation, Sexual harassment, etc. There are some acts too, at your service, like the Maternity Benefit Act, the Dowry Prohibition Act, the Medical Termination of Pregnancy Act, the Criminal Law Act, the Indecent Representation of Women

(Prohibition) Act, the Protection of Women from Domestic Violence Act, and many more. You can even get help from the National Commission for Women."

She murmured, in a confused state, "I am not good at understanding these. But it seems you have very good knowledge in this topic. "

I replied in fun, "Don't worry. It is just due to a lack of experience. The more time you will spend with your spouse, the more you will learn, and I am lucky enough and thankful to my wife as she taught me so much about this which I was never aware of."

For the first time since we started our discussion, it made both of us laugh. I was laughing at my pity situation, and maybe she was laughing at my miserable life. I have accepted my fate and have stopped cursing my life. Rather, I try to enjoy each moment of it as there is no use in wasting my blessed life due to my current situation. Time never stops. If it is a bad day now, I am confident that good days are waiting for me too. Life is never smooth; it has its ups and downs, but it depends on me how I deal with the situation and surf through the tough time as a winner without getting drowned in it.

There was a silence between us after a long time; I was lost in my thoughts, looking outside the window, observing things passing by at the high speed of the train. Trees, poles, and stations all passed by in a few seconds, similar to the condition of my life. All the happiness, ease, and relief that I used to have once upon a time in my life had gone away in a snap. I thought I would enjoy and have a very happy life ahead of marriage. I imagined having a companion for life with me as my partner in crime, as a friend with whom I would share all my happiness and sorrows. We will both be each other's pillars of strength, but somebody has rightly said that you should never make plans as they never happen the way you always wish them to happen.

I heard a voice bringing me back to my present pathetic time from the good old imaginary world, asking me, "What about men?"

I said, "Sorry."

She replied, "I mean to say, what about men? What laws are there to protect men against crime?"

I replied on a lighter note, in a witty way, "I hope your brain has not started planning to sue your would-be. Anyways, surprisingly, we are not protected by any law, as it may be because legislation or our government assumes that men are only criminals and no man is ever a sufferer, or that we are strong enough to bear what all happens to us, or we can say that maybe we are made to bear all the tortures and never react to any sort of pain. You may feel pity for us that we don't even have a National Men's Commission for us."

She interrupted me, saying, "But why? If I remember it correctly, you only said something about the right to equality. So, if women have it, even men should have it. Because any human being can suffer, and they need a helping hand for themselves to pull them out of the mud. "

I said, with a light smile on my face, "I wish everyone would have thought the same way you are thinking. Well, it's indeed high time that the government thinks about bringing in the National Men's Commission to support men in this crisis. It has become a basic necessity for every man to have a respectable and stress-free life. I just wish that the sun of hope would rise during my lifetime itself, and I could see every man feeling liberated from the unnecessary stress of fake accusations. I could not understand what was stopping them from bringing this in for the noble cause.

The government is only focusing on making women centric laws and, in the name of the laws to bring gender equality, is paving the way for more inequality towards the male gender through gender-biased schemes and programmes just to please the women vote bank. If this is going to continue, soon no male will be left alive to vote for them."

Suddenly, she jumped in between, saying, "Don't worry at all. I have full faith in my government and the honourable Supreme Court. When they can take such big decisions like bringing in the triple talaq bill, taking a strong stand on the Ayodhya case, revoking Article 370, they surely will do good for men too, as every society needs balance, which is created by the existence and well-being of every gender. Even in the Bhagavad Gita, Krishna says that "whenever and wherever there is a decay of righteousness, for the protection of the good and the destruction of evil-doers, the gods will bear witness for the sake of establishing righteousness firmly." It means that the right thing will reach good and innocent people in some way."

I said, with a sigh, "Yes, but it should not get late. Do you know that, as per the National Crime Records Bureau (NCRB), we lost 1,18,979 men to suicide in 2021 whereas in 2019 it was 97613? The overall male : female ratio of suicide victims for the year 2021 was 72.5 : 27.4, which is more as compared to the last year 2020. The MSI, which is the ratio of male to female suicides in India, has increased by approximately 52% in the past 20 years, whereas the population growth over the same period, i.e., between 2000 and 2019, is only about 28%. And you won't believe that since 1967, there has been an increase from 1.4 to 2.35, or in layman's terms, I can say that for every 100 females in India who commit suicide, 235 men commit suicide. The latest National Crime Records Bureau (NCRB) report reveals data on the suicide victims by age and sex group states that the women & men suicide victims' ratio is 1:1 till 18 years and it rises to 1:5 in 45-60 years. Now, everything you've been told so far has been about men and women in general as a gender. Let's focus on the data of the Husband Suicide Index (HSI), i.e., the ratio of married male suicides to married female suicides in India, which shows that 66815 married men were lost to suicide, which shows an increase of 3.1 % as compared to the 6.5% decrease in suicides of married women. If you look back over the past 20 years, you will be surprised to know that HSI has increased by 61%. The year 2019 is the saddest year for all of us as it has recorded the steepest jump in HSI since 1995. And family problems are the most common reason given for suicide, accounting for 32.4% of all suicides. Again the data shows that the rate of committing suicide among married men is three times that of married women. In 2021 as many as 81063 married men committed suicide while the women's figure stood at 28660. Surprisingly, in the case of divorced and separated men, they are about 8% less likely to commit suicide as compared to married people, whereas women show an increase of about 8%in their ratio of total suicides as compared to the married population."

I must say that this girl was full of patience. Listening to the whole conversation of mine submissively, she said, "OMG, how could you remember all the data? I am surprised. You must be very intelligent. Can I ask, what have you studied? And sorry, I forgot to ask your name too. If you don't mind, can you please introduce yourself?"

I laughed and replied, "My introduction for these many hours is not enough for you. Well, never mind. Earlier, I was introduced as *Raja Karwa*, B. Tech., M. Tech., Ph.D. from IIT Kharagpur, but now the introduction is changed to

Raja Karwa, IPC 125, IPC 498a, IPC 377, DVA, IPC 406, IPC 504, IPC 506, IPC section 3/4 Dowry, IPC 342, IPC 354, IPC 383, IPC 386, IPC 467, IPC 468, IPC 471, IPC420."

Astonishingly, she said, "OMG, what does IPC stand for? I am really getting puzzled with all these numbers."

Replying in jest, I said, "You are lucky. You don't need to look into these numbers as the government has protection for you. These are merely for men. Well, these are all the Indian Penal Code sections, or rather accusations, imposed on me by my loving wife as a lifetime gift in exchange for the petty family issues between us that could have been resolved, and as I was not able to live up to her expectations, as she dreamt of having a fairy-tale life post marriage, which was beyond the practical and real-life truths. With the intention of spoiling, you and your loved one's lives, they will try their best to manipulate you from day one. If they realise that their husband is not doing what they are wishing, soon she will be filled with ego and, with the feeling of revenge, she will file 'n' number of cases against you with the intention of spoiling you and your loved one's life."

"I feel pity for such boys and men. My mind is just trying to think about the possibilities. Why does the beautiful, pious relationship end up in divorce?" she said inadvertently.

XIII

For a while, I became silent, not because I wasn't aware of the answer, but just because I was not able to understand how to frame the answer and present it to her, as there is not just one reason but thousands of reasons, including those people who act as catalysts and pretend to be your well-wisher and saviour. They provoke you despite resolving the problems by increasing the rate of a reaction within you by boiling your blood more. They will make you to take wrong steps against your spouse by interfering in your personal life without themselves undergoing any permanent changes, as your life hardly matters to them and your agony becomes the talk of the town for them.

As an answer to her question, I replied, "In recent years, a persistent surge in the number of divorce cases has been observed. We are proud to be Indian, but unfortunately, deep-rooted cultural values and customs are becoming a lack lustre display due to modern beliefs, high ambitions, materialistic thoughts, never-compromising or adjusting attitudes, and superiority /inferiority complexes among spouses. An Indian marriage, from once being considered as the companionship of every birth, has seen a transformation to hardly withstanding each other even for a single month. These are all the reflections of the social, economic, emotional, and psychological changes that are most commonly considered as the up gradation of the lifestyle by many people who are high on ego and want to show themselves on par with the western influence. There is a chain reaction happening in the relationship as well, which usually starts with a difference in the mindset of the two, leading to the differences causing a lack of love, respect, and understanding for each other. There are many factors for divorce, such as cruelty, adultery, desertion, leprosy, venereal disease, mental disorder, acceptance of religious order on renouncing the world, the respondent had not heard of being alive for seven years, conversion to some other religion, sentence of imprisonment for seven years, no resumption of cohabitation, incompatibility, non-disclosure of facts, forced marriage, etc. But the greatest danger of all is parental or sibling interference. Well, do you know Newton's second law?"

"Yes, I understand," she grumbled, "but where has Newton entered this discussion? Did he even face domestic violence and false cases against him?"

I laughed and said, 'No.'

And I started explaining to her, "Newton's second law says that when a constant force acts on a massive body, it causes it to accelerate, or we can say that a force applied to an object at rest causes it to accelerate in the direction of the force.

However, if the object is already in motion, its body might appear to speed up, slow down, or change direction depending upon the direction of the force. So, to your surprise, the same law is applicable to marriages too."

She replied, "Yes, but how is it relevant?"

To which I replied, " F= ma, so here, (Greek letter sigma) represents the vector sum of all the forces, acting on a body.

Here, F, i.e., the force acting on an object could be the misguided or unethical lessons taught by some parents to their daughter's which acts as the net force which does not let the girl accept or adjust to the family, which starts from not cooperating with the in-laws and their members, making the husband your slave, doing as per her wish, never compromising attitude, making your own nuclear family sans in-laws, and the list is never-ending. So, when the external force is so high, it's definite for the body (wife) to flow in their direction.

Now as per the second condition, where the object is already in motion. If l compare the second condition with marriage, I will relate it as, if the wife already has the mind set of adamancy and arrogance with no compromising agenda and similar is fed to her, she will either try to separate the husband from his family from the first day of marriage or separate herself from her husband citing incompatibility issues from day one itself. I would rather say that the mind set of the wife is directly proportional to the direction she chooses to follow. Either she will create a happy family or she will do everything she can to end up in a divorce and screw up the unlucky person who got involved with her."

"Oh my god, how well you relate the matrimonial issues with the subjects and laws, which I never thought would be of any use ever in my life," she said in a wittier way, with a laugh.

I responded by saying, "Whatever you learn in life will never go to waste. And the suffering in me has made me relate to anything and everything around me with this, as I kept on searching for the reason for my suffering. "

"Don't feel bad, but you look so intelligent, understanding, generous, humorous, fun-loving and you are not bad in your looks either. What else would a girl wish to have? I don't understand why or what could be the reason for your estranged wife to drag you or what could be the story of your marital discord?" she asked eagerly.

There was a curiosity in her voice while asking me my story, so sensing the inquisitiveness I replied, "If this was the scene, then Hrithik Roshan would never have gotten divorced.

To date, what I have learnt about the girls is that they are hardcore believers in the phrase 'The grass is always greener on the other side.' No matter how good person their partners are, they are never satisfied and always crave for rest. For them, rest is best, and the one that they have should be treated as a slave. My story is no different than any other couple in dispute. Every other person who is indulged in a matter similar to mine always starts with a very minute argument similar to a spark, which ends up in a huge fire burning the whole forest of this relationship, including the pretty flowers, which resemble the good happy times that we have spent together, while bushes, shrubs, and creepers signify the tough times, arguments, disagreements, and fights that we have had during our tenure."

She slipped into deep thought and, upon asking, she randomly replied, saying, "Court is a big thing to happen in one's life. How could some girl belonging to an esteemed and reputable family dare to step in and even think of doing so, as because if she is dragging you, she will have to come on the ground to face such things? If it's fora genuine cause, then it's perfectly fine. I would also support her in taking such drastic step, but if it is about false allegations, then I must say she should have the guts to do so. I don't know what kind of moral values she bears, which makes her to lie and drag the other party to court and harass herself by doing the same too?"

I murmured, "Who can better understand the answer to this question than the one who himself got stuck in this muddy instance?"

She asked me, in a very low voice, "What happens in the courtroom when she faces you?" Does she continue cooking up stories and blaming you? I mean, what happens in the courtroom during divorce proceedings? Who ultimately wins? Do they succeed by mere lying or does the judge get to know the hidden truth and give away justice to the right one?"

As a reply to her answer, I said, "There is no question of winning and losing here. Whoever wins is even a loser. Even if the girl wins the case and is successful in blaming and claiming false allegations against the boy, she will still lose her battle to have a happy life with her partner and a successful marriage. The same goes with boys; even if he wins and becomes successful in proving himself innocent and trashing all the allegations claimed by his wife, he still loses the battle to have a happily ever after-life. Well, in the courtroom, both parties carry with them a big bag full of mud, shit, stones, and pebbles and keep on throwing them at each other just to prove they are right, with no plans ever to sit down and chat and resolve the issues. Who doesn't have misunderstandings or disagreements with their spouse, parents and their son or daughter, or siblings, but do these relationships also end up in divorce, dragging each other to court? Marriages are no longer a sacred relationship. In today's era, I would say that it is the weakest relationship of all. If you don't feel like living with your partner, or if your ego gets hurt, just break the relationship by divorcing each other and drag them to court has become a common practice. Make sure that you harass the guy in every possible way. Do not dare skip any sections in order to put blame on him. The fight is ego (female) vs ego (male) and more than this, it is the ego of 4, i.e., the ego of a girl's mother, father, sister, and brother vs. boy's ego. They all plan together to take revenge on you and make your life hell. Marriage has become a fun game now to extort money by playing the blame game. They can't withstand husbands, but they can withstand their earnings, the jewellery gifted to them by the groom's side, and all the materialistic things in the world. I sometimes feel that this is the best job ever. You don't have to struggle to earn; no work, no pressure of balancing with anyone in the family, no liabilities, no responsibilities, and you still earn monthly maintenance just by claiming false allegations and dragging men to court. As soon as they enter the courtroom, the pious relationship becomes a venomous one. The scope of mending ever in a lifetime comes to an end with no or little hope left. "

And she suddenly interrupted me, saying, "Hey, what is a no-fault divorce?" I have come across this word but have no idea about it. Can you please brief me about it?"

I continued explaining to her again, "Well, a no-fault divorce is the one where the spouse who demands a divorce does not have to prove the other guilty, but presently Indian law does not recognise it, but only the Supreme Court does it with a distinct nomenclature calling it as an irretrievable breakdown of marriage, like in the case where the apex court is convinced beyond any doubt that there is actually no chance of the marriage surviving and it is broken beyond repair, but after years of legal battles. Well, I would say that it has failed in India."

To which she uttered quickly, "Oh, it seems there is the least possibility of opting for a no-fault divorce,"

Taking a small pause, she continued, "in which nobody spoils each other's image, time, or life," (she said in a very thoughtful and low voice.)

"No, not at all, as the girl's side will not let you have a no-fault divorce ever because that won't satisfy their inner soul. The girl and her family usually become happy to see you unhappy," I replied.

She said, "I always thought that females are the beautiful creations of God with so much love in them. They bear a heart of gold, thoughts like glittering diamonds, bright as silver, calm as the moon."

And I laughed and interrupted her, saying, "Alas, that might be correct, but I had the fate of encountering a woman who had dreams of being loaded with gold, diamonds, and silver, and yup, she was as calm as the moon by creating high tides in my life as well as in my family member's life. Whatever I did to her, she was never satisfied and always compared me with her friend's husband, her father, or any of the male members to her knowledge. I have my own identity, but, in her presence, I started feeling as if my wings were tied up, and I lost my own identity, being faceless. I was always judged at home, which is a place where you can relax and be who you are. I can't even express myself to anybody, not even my wife, as she never understood my feelings and conditions and used my situation to bitch about me to her parents. It all suffocated me, but still, I did not have any option to untie myself. People say that a girl leaves everything for you, and it's the boy's responsibility to make the girl happy. But leaving materialistic things is even easier for us too as because she doesn't compromise, but rather keeps pestering us to buy new things for her. Moreover, she always compares her life before marriage with the present one. She hardly leaves any pre-marital relationships, but rather forces the boy to maintain a relationship with her whole family wholeheartedly and makes him leave his own family. If at any time the boy is not in a good mood and does not entertain her family, the boy must be ready to bear the thrash of all his in-laws through your wife, and you will be gifted with a long list of allegations that were never ever committed by you."

XIV

She replied, "I really feel hurt knowing all this about females. The females were considered so pious in their behaviour and thought. So many goddesses exist who have done so much for good and have become victorious over all evil, spreading positivity, faith, and goodness all around. Since when have these kinds of girls started coming into existence?"

"Since when?" I replied, interrupting her. Surprisingly, she looked at me with no clue about what I had just told her.

I answered saying, "Since ages Haven't you heard of various mythological stories about *Rakhshasis? There* existed a female version of evil spirits too in all the yugas. "And looking at her, I laughed.

She got perplexed and said, "Will you again make an effort to explain this to me?"

And I happily continued, "Have you ever heard of *Putna, Tadaka, Shurpanakha, Lankini, Surasa,* and many more? These were women who, under the shadow of being a woman, did all the evil acts and tried to harm people around them. *Putna* tried to kill *Krishna* by breastfeeding poisoned milk. *Tadaka,* used to harass and attack *rishis* performing yajnas. There are many more never ending stories of female *rakshasis*. Wasn't that a heinous crime committed by females against males? Regardless of gender, anyone can be good or bad. It's not always that men should be tagged as wrong. The above examples are to make you realise that even female demons existed in the olden days and still exist and are even easy to find around you if you stop differentiating between the genders and do not fall for their cooked-up stories and crocodile tears."

She asserted, "Yes, you are right, but I think it has gone to our blood to consider that women are always right and men are always wrong, and I think that it is really going to get difficult for everybody to shift their view from gender bias to gender unbiasedness."

We were tongue-tied for a moment, and I got exhausted explaining it, as it is a never-ending topic to talk about. But I could sense that she was having a good brainstorm within her.

In a thoughtful voice, she asked me, "Is it really not possible to have a no-fault divorce? I mean, if two people are not comfortable with each other, they could opt for an amicable separation.

Every soul has the right to have their piece of peace."

"As I have already said, it is mainly, mostly, and merely the fight of the three-letter word, 'EGO.'" I replied, trying to add a bit of humour to it, but it seemed she was not in the mood to take up the humor, so I replied in a serious tone, "The main reason most women drag men to court is that it gives them a sense of satisfaction to harass men, and they enjoy seeing men destroyed as in the case of Tadaka. We men generally forget, but women have God-gifted sharp brain to remember all the faults of their spouses with the date and time, even if the spouse did not commit the fault intentionally."

She asked inadvertently, "What is your story of matrimonial discord?"

I said, "Surprisingly, you will always find two versions of matrimonial discord. One is the female version, and the other is the male version. And to your surprise, most of the females have similar kinds of charges and complaints against their husbands. "

And she interrupted, saying, "Similar? I mean, how is that possible?"

I replied, "Yes, all the complaints are as per the available list of accusations, which every family lawyer and criminal lawyer keeps with them. It's more like a menu card, and you just have to choose the one that you like and start mentioning as in *a la carte*. It's as easy as that. But the toughest job is for men when compared to women. Men have zero laws in their favour, making them the worst sufferers on this planet. These days, legal rights given to women for their protection have become a joke of the town as every woman uses this right to instigate men, even in a lighter or fun-filled mood.

There is a comedy show which runs on an Indian television channel where one of the renowned cricketers, who is also a politician, was invited along with his wife, where his wife jokingly said to him, "If you ever try to torture me, then I will call the cops and get you arrested." Surprisingly, everybody present on the show, including the cricketer, started laughing loudly. Until it is a joke, it is fine, but when most women start using it as a sharp weapon to assassinate the character and image of their husbands or men by calling the police and throwing up the lies at them, it becomes worse for the male gender. Many real-life stories are existing since many eras, where women have misused the law; which was given to them to protect themselves, by raping men."

Surprisingly, she interrupted me, asking, "Rape men by women? How is that even possible?" I replied, "Well, to your information, rape is a Latin word meaning to snatch, to grab, to carry off, or to seize or take away by force. Rape is categorised as a crime against humanity. Men are being raped legally by their wives, or 'women', the so-called weaker sex, by exercising their power on their husbands and using actual force or the threat of it to take control of their husbands by using enacted laws and misusing state machinery to snatch, to grab, to carry off, or to seize or take away by force. Rape is categorised as a crime against humanity.

Both have the same impact. We men are no different than women. If using the right given by the Indian constitution for threatening somebody and still being safe is a woman's right, then women don't deserve these laws. Women's rights are given for protection, and these days women are using them as a shield to make the victim sound like the culprit. Well, I don't blame girls; rather, I would blame the dreamy world gifted by our so-called great Bollywood. They have created irrational expectations in girls. It's very easy for the directors of the movie to show the love blossoming between the rich and the poor. The heroine will be running behind the poor hero, but in reality, they will only get married to a rich person. If they don't follow it, then why do they incorporate such thoughts into the tender mind?

Similarly, in real life, actors fail to create a romantic bond 24x7 as shown in movies. Sometimes I get surprised watching them show love, concern, and care towards the actress in the movie, and I could see them together throughout the movie, spending heavily on the actress and giving her surprises, taking her on foreign trips, and having servants all around. I mean, at what time of the day or night do they work to earn so much to give the other half all the amenities? In real life, we either earn or enjoy. It becomes very hectic and only a few lucky people will have the opportunity to enjoy both. If I could relate it to my life, I spend almost 12 hours a day in the office, 3 hours daily traveling, 6 hours of sleep, which is highly required by the body and brain to function normally, and the 3 hours that are left are used for managing the tantrums of my wife. Although I earn well, I never get enough time for myself. I made every possible effort to make her happy and satisfied, but her expectations and comparisons had no limits. Everything that I did for her never made her happy, and I was always on the scale of comparison. Every person needs words of appreciation. Always commenting on the husband, indirectly indulging his family members, his virtues, his earnings do even come under mental torture by the wife. Is it not against the law of nature that only the female gender suffers mental trauma and no males suffer the same as indicated by the law? When *rakshasis* of the olden eras are living examples, then why does the law refuse the truth that the men are being mentally tortured? Rather, I would say that it is more difficult for men to balance everything around them. A girl simply leaves her house and enters the new world and feels harassed by not being able to adjust or cope with the new environment, whereas men are neglected on this topic as they are more pressured to balance.

I would say it's similar to walking on a rope for men. Once he gets married, if he utters anything out of his mouth that is against the wishes of his parents or siblings, soon there will be a round table conference taking place sans the boy declaring, "Look! Marriage has brought so many changes in him. He is not bothered for us. He is now a henpecked man." And to my wife, I am a 'mama's boy'. You are not just bound to take care of your own family and members, but you have to take more care of your wife and her family members than you do of your own parents, as your wife will always keep a sharp eye on you. Even if you give or do your best for your in-laws, you will be underestimated until your last breath, and you must be wondering what you did wrong to them that enraged your wife. In fact, I must tell you, preparing for IIT and further studying at IIT was much easier for me than understanding the psychology of a woman. If you don't give them enough time, they will complain not just to you but to everybody that their daughter's husband ignores her. And, if you think you take time out of your busy schedule for her to make her happy and work on the complaints, you will be judged as 'a man without any work'. Say, you ask your wife for some outing, and she will refuse, citing some reason or excuse. Whereas, if you don't find time for her, you will be blamed for having an extramarital affair at the office or other places.

Dealing with the boss and the office is never easy. It is so difficult to survive in today's competitive world; everyone in the office is there to pull you down. You are always under pressure to give your best to get a good appraisal and a promotion. Guess for whom? Yes, for you and your loved ones, especially to make her feel proud and demonstrate her worth. But surprisingly, if you stay for more than 3 years in the same organization, assuming a future ahead and as per your good plans, you will be tagged as inefficient to get a good opportunity with another organization with a good increment. And if you keep on changing jobs, you will be tagged as not serious or not stable at anything in life, nor even mentally. I never asked, forced, or commented ever on my wife's job. She has been working there for a long time. I was glad to see her happy, but I had no idea that one day a lawsuit would be filed against me, claiming that I was too bossy and continued to control her.

Instead, I was the one who slowly became a rolling stone for her, who started moving in the direction she liked. Before marriage she said that she would never quit her job. I even loved an independent woman, so I never asked her to do so, but I was blamed, stating that I was greedy. So, hearing that one day while having a conversation with her, I politely told her, "*Rani*, if you don't want to work, quit it. I don't like seeing you stressed. Do I not earn enough to fulfil all your needs and wishes?"

But to my surprise, she replied to me in a harsh tone, saying, "You are bossy *Raja*, too dominating, and want me to borrow your legs, and follow you wherever you direct me. I know you intend to hire me as a maid and secure your home's four perimeter walls. Since, your father has become ill, you want me to be a caretaker and maid for your older parents. I am a girl of a new generation and would never fall into your trap. I have my senses and my brain to decide what is best for me in the future."

After listening to her views, I was surprised and totally stunned and could not utter a single word. I realised that even if I think for her benefit, she will judge all of my actions negatively. I was the one chosen for the marriage because of my good package and profile by *Rani*'s family. They wanted to settle their daughter's financial insecurities, but still, the dowry case is running on me without even asking for a single penny from her family. We were very open-minded and were always against the dowry system, as

I do have a sister, and we married her off to a person who did not demand even a single penny. And by god's grace, she is happy too. The bride's side is greedy too, but I am shocked to see that the law considers the groom's side only greedy. We did not ask for a single penny, but soon after our marriage was fixed, my mother in-law started calling my mother asking how many gold-sets and gifts she would give to her daughter. Isn't that a crime? We got many things for the bride as my parents had desired, but still, I was always taunted by my wife and in-laws that we got everything substandard for her, and she even said that they felt like throwing them away. Isn't that a crime? She was about to abort my child as she never wanted to get pregnant early, and throughout the pregnancy, I was blamed for it. My mom made her understand that kids are the gift of God and not to abort them.

However, she put the blame on us for trying to abort our baby. When my father got severely ill and we shifted to my parent's house, she did not leave any stone unturned to stress the situation more and left the place without informing anybody. We did not mind then either, but she did not stop here. She left for her house without even informing me and stopped picking up my phone. I was already in a very traumatic situation, and she made it worse by giving me unnecessary stress. I don't know why the law becomes blind when it comes to the matter of discord between husband and wife, or male and female.

Why does it blindly listen to women and completely ignore men? Are we made up of steel? Usually, most of the complaints are filed in the heat of the moment over trivial issues. I have observed that instead of settling the issue and preventing the house of their daughter from breaking, parents prefer to fuel and fan the matter by provoking their own daughter never to compromise, stating that she is equally educated as the boy, so why should she adjust to the boy whereas he puts all his efforts to mend up things. In fact, he devotes all of his energy to console and adjust to the situation. However, things worsen when the other party refuses to mend and thrashes you with threats of incarceration."

XV

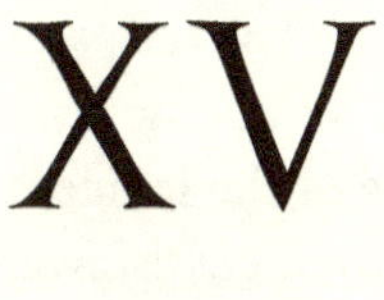

This just does not only happen between husband and wife; rather, there are several real life examples where the boys have to suffer because girls have become smarter in utilising them and throwing them away when girls don't need them anymore. There are several cases which you might have heard about on news channels and social media, leaving no stone unturned to make the girl a superwoman and spoil the image of a boy to such an extent that it often becomes impossible to regain the lost image. If modesty is a woman's jewel, then I must say that modesty is the complete attire of men as well. When a woman drags our esteem to the roadside and publicly criticises us for our no-fault, we are made to stand nude and struggle hard to find even a grain to cover us. Maybe for women, it is fun, but it is no fun for us who have put our all-time energy and efforts into building regard and respect towards ourselves, which within no time is easily spoiled by the other party.

Have you ever heard of the *Jasleen Kaur* harassment controversy?

"Yeah, the one where the boy misbehaved with the girl on a busy traffic crossing", she replied.

To which, I said, refusing her statement, "No, the part which was highlighted by the media was all the false story cooked up by the girl. The truth was not disclosed to the society in a proper way. So, most of the people know the half-truth. This is one of the incidents that shows the true side of a society where a girl is awarded with cash prizes for cooking up false stories and a boy is punished in jail because he was not able to stand the wrath of the ego and show-off of a girl. Everybody else, without being an eyewitness to the incident, blindly believed the false story cooked up by the girl. Now, that's the power of being a girl, and society calls them 'the weaker sex.' Post that she was made a super heroine for raising her voice against eve-teasing and sexual harassment on social media, whereas the boy was labelled as 'National Pervert' and 'Delhi ka Darinda' (Delhi's predator). I still remember how the news anchors were chasing him and were trying to prove him guilty by using inappropriate words against him. Soon, the girl was lauded with praise and was even awarded with a cash reward of 5000 rupees, whereas *Saravjeet* was sent to jail, which was his reward for being a male and being respectable towards the female. Actually, in that incident *Saravjeet* was driving and in fact was following the traffic rules, he did not initiate any conversation with that girl. Rather, she intervened with him and tried to stop him from taking a left turn, which was a free turn as per traffic rules, but still he was the one who had to suffer.

Yes, it was 'HE,' the gender 'HE.' She left Delhi and flew abroad, not turning back for next 03 years, citing her 'academic commitments' never to attend even a single session of the court, consequently, making *Saravjeet* suffer, as he was the one who attended all the 14 sessions of the court. While she found it hard to take time out of her studies, *Saravjeet* was struggling to keep a job here. *Saravjeet* was the one who was at loss and lost his precious 4 years along with his job, mental peace and many more shortly after this incident. He had struggled through this period. But as said, the "truth prevails"; soon after it came in front of everybody, he was freed from all charges and held innocent. And later, the court observed, "It is pertinent to mention that there are various contradictions and improvements in the version of the complainants... The complainant has made material improvements to her statements. In view of the same, the testimony of the complainant is not trustworthy and casts a serious doubt on the case of the prosecution". My question is, what actions were taken against that girl? Was she punished for fabricating the story and damaging someone's image and spoiling his life? Was she ever imprisoned? The answer is 'NO' and I must say that this is the power of being a 'SHE'. Even though many laws exist through which they can be punished, she escaped it well. This real-life example shows how false cases can ruin one's life. Maybe blaming a guy was very easy and fun for her, but before doing such an act, had she ever thought of her brother, father, etc.? We boys, on the other hand are instructed by our parents to think of our own sisters and mothers before being rude or saying anything to any girl. The same lesson should be taught to girls by their parents to behave properly with boys in this 21st century."

"Oh, is it that? I never knew the second half of the story. Nor even was aware that he was proved innocent by our honourable supreme court. I am surprised to find this story where the girl was at fault." She said promptly.

I laughed at the pity condition of men and continued, "This is not just one. There are many real-life incidences. Let me tell you one more story of another innocent man named *Munish Dalal* who got trapped in an anti-dowry lawsuit by a clever and smart girl called *Nisha Sharma* in the year 2003. This real-life story is a perfect example of how the IPC 498A law can be misused. This honest man lost 9 years of his precious life. There are never-ending life-ruining stories, and similarly, the new ones are still in the making due to the wrong implementation of laws. This marriage was arranged by the parents of both families after meeting each other a few times. Finally, the catastrophic night of their marriage arrived, where he was made 'guilty until proven innocent' as per the Indian criminal justice system. Stories were fabricated and false cases were filed against him, his mother, and his relatives by *Nisha* for demanding 12 lakh rupees in cash and a Maruti Esteem car from the bride's father by the groom's mother, along with verbal abuses. Thereafter, a scuffle broke out between the two, and every wrong act as per the bride and her family was done by the groom's side only, and hearing all this, *Nisha* called the cops and made them arrested, whereas the true story revealed was totally different. *Munish* claimed that they never did any kind of verbal abuse, nor even raised any demand or initiated any fight with the bride's father. Rather, they were surprised to learn the real story behind the suspicious act of the bride's family, as they were delaying the ritual of reaching the bride's house with the procession, which is usually welcomed by the members of the bride's family. After a long wait, a guy named Navneet came to the groom's place, and he claimed that he was the lover and had been in a relationship with her for five years. He even claimed himself to be the husband of *Nisha*. Hearing this, the bride's father got angry and he initiated the spat by hitting the groom's mother with a sandal. Her father admitted that

Navneet wanted to marry *Nisha*, but he was unemployed. The whole fault was of *Nisha*, as she didn't want to marry *Munish* but was scared of his parents, so she made *Munish* suffer for her actions by accusing him falsely of getting out of the marriage, exceeding the anger of her parents. *Munish* not only lost his job along with his reputation. He was not the only one at loss; rather, his widow mother, who was a school teacher, also lost her job and was denied of her retirement benefits. *Nisha* completely utilised the power of being female and utilised the legal provisions made for the betterment of real-suffering women at their best. The benefits that *Nisha* earned out of this incident were numerous and something that people crave. She became a celebrity overnight with the help of the media. She appeared on the front pages of several newspapers. She was interviewed by several media people day and night and was congratulated by several high-profile people. She was even invited to contest the local election. This false story was covered by both the national and international media. She was even captured in an Amul Butter Girl cartoon. Surprisingly, she was even invited by Oprah Winfrey to her talk show, where she went along with her husband and brother. This was not the end of the illusionary glory that she had been receiving during those days. She was even included in the English textbook for Class 6 by the State Council of Educational Research and Training of the New Delhi region, in the form of a chapter titled 'Man in Jail over Dowry Demand'. She barely attended 10 sessions of the court trials, whereas *Munish* and his innocent family members were arrested. The chapter that was included in the book had a very negative impact on the life of the groom's mother, as it was taught in the same school where she had retired as a teacher, and it ruined her reputation completely, resulting in her being denied her pension and retirement benefits. He and his family members were the ones who needed to attend all the trials in court. While awaiting trial in the jail, he was assaulted by his fellow inmates, who called him 'a greedy groom.' As a result, *Munish* suffered many injuries. The mound of grief that a person bears when his image or reputation is ruined by someone else when he is young has no comparison. Materialistic things can be regained, but self-esteem, once lost, is lost, and is very difficult to rebuild, no matter how much you try. This stigma stays with you till your last breath. To my surprise, *Nisha* was depicted as a heroic figure, but in 2012, when the verdict came and *Munish* was acquitted along with Navneet (her boyfriend), who was accused of forging the marriage documents, which could not be proven to be forged by the prosecution. The worst part about this case was that none of the media, activists, or politicians provided any statement after the court acquitted the accused in the false case.

The problem with the law's revealing only the man's name is that it can also ruin an innocent man's life. Although the true men's community is all surrounded by trouble and injustice, I still believe in karma. Karma will take its own account of the faulty and sinful people who pretend to be very smart and try to harass the other party without their fault. The Karma web is stronger than any kind of web existing in the world."

"Karma web? What is that? I have never heard of it. That sounds interesting. Can you please take the pain again to explain this to me?", asked the girl.

I replied, "Well, the karma web is a web that traps everyone in such a way that it becomes impossible for them to get away from it. And I am sure that it is not sympathetic based on any gender, as karma is unbiased and acts as per their actions which they have performed throughout their life. The problem with us is that we love to listen and talk about religious things and would love to listen to the preaching of the religious gurus. We will preach good, great saintly thoughts to everybody, but when it comes to ourselves, we fail to obey, as an individual, what we preach to others. The moment they leave the preaching place, they forget what they were taught and start pulling each other's legs and pushing others in the mud."

After a brief silence, "Do you have a paper?" I asked her.

She got startled and started searching for one and handed me over one sheet. I tore half the page and returned her the other half.

She said, "That's fine, you can use the sheet. I don't need the other half of it back.

I replied, "We should never waste our resources," and I started writing something on my sheet. After I finished writing, I showed it to her.

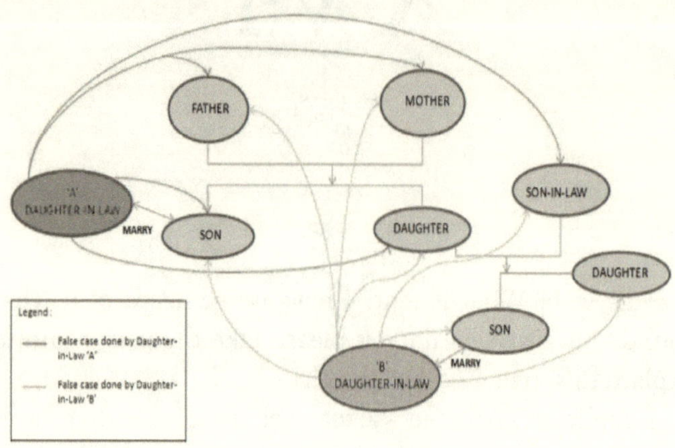

Looking at it, she gave me a puzzled look and asked me, "What is it?"

I replied to her, saying, "This is the vicious circle of the Karma web."

"Vicious circle?" Surprisingly, she asked me I said, "Yes, the vicious circle that never ends, keeps on going, and has no end to it.

Usually, females consider themselves safe and get a feeling of the protection layer surrounding them in the form of many legal rights provided to them or several women's commissions which stand for them. But to my surprise, these so-called women oriented rights are not even in favour of them. Some daughters-in-law and their mothers blackmail the groom and his relatives to sue them in court and enjoy taking benefits out of it. Shortcut benefits may always lure you or you may feel as if you are on cloud 9 by cheating and extorting the weaker and innocent ones by threatening them, but always remember that karma is not blind. He is following you everywhere and is noting down each of your evil acts and is ready to punish you at any time in life. "

"Yes, I understood this all, but will you please explain this vicious circle to me?" She asked me in haste, interrupting me.

I continued, "Oh yes, I just skipped it in the flow of my talk. So, what I have drawn here is a happy family where a couple had a daughter and a son, but one day their bad time started when their son got married. So, since the stars were not in favour of them, they were unlucky in welcoming a daughter-in-law who kept pestering, torturing, and threatening to sue them in court by registering a false complaint against them at the police station to teach them a lesson as they were not following or listening to her. So, one day, she goes out and traps everybody in false cases. Now, karma gets into the action. It doesn't believe in giving quick justice, but even though it will take many years to deliver justice, some way or the other, the wrong doer will definitely get entangled in the same web created by him/her."

"But how?" she asked.

I took another piece of paper and drew one more representation and showed it to her and started explaining,

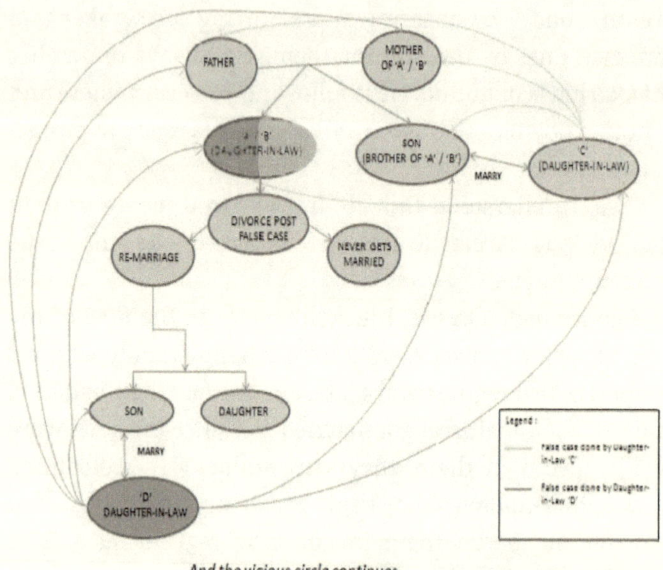

...And the vicious circle continues

"You must have heard that 'Karma is a bitch'. Karma is the idea that if you do bad things, bad things will happen to you. If you do good things, good things will happen to you. A similar case exists everywhere. In the above representation, you can see how daughters-in law, rather than living happily with their family, enjoy trapping the other party in false cases and harassing husbands and their relatives, which include elderly people too, until their last breath. Now, in the second representation, I will show you that karma takes revenge on the culprits for their bad actions, and it also takes revenge on them. Let's see the picture representation of the other side of how the culprit daughter-in-law can get into the trap of the web which was created by her own. After getting divorced from her husband and getting a hefty amount of alimony, she has two options: either she remarries or she will never marry. She could be trapped in both cases. Let us see how? Suppose she has a brother and her brother gets married, and his brother's wife puts a case on him and simultaneously on the rest of the family members, she automatically gets into the trap.

Suppose she escapes, maybe because her planetary motions are in her favor, but there are many incidences where she can get trapped. If she remarries and has a son and a daughter in the future, maybe after a long time, she may still get trapped in this web when her son gets married. There is even a possibility that after her daughter gets married and she marries off her son, that daughter-in-law may even do the required act as supported by our legal system. And this vicious circle keeps on continuing like this forever and ever. The living example of this is *Nisha*. "

"*Nisha*?? Who *Nisha*??", she said interrupting me.

I replied, "*Nisha* and *Munish*, whose story I narrated to you a few hours back,"

"Oh yes, I could recall that now. Sorry for interrupting you. Please continue. How did Karma take its revenge on *Nisha* for her wrongful act? " She asked curiously.

To quench her curiosity, I continued, "Her sister-in-law filed a complaint against her husband and *Nisha* for demanding Rs. 12,00,000 and beating her up for that in 2013."

"Oh my God! I am surprised. So, soon she got trapped in the web of karma for her actions. The next year, after *Munish* was acquitted of all the charges, 'God is great,'" she said in a happy tone. Hearing to the link which she created and the optimistic conclusion, I said, "Yes, but surprisingly, there was no media coverage, no hype on this matter, which would have taken this news to each person as they did in 2003 to spoil *Munish*'s image. But at least it gives me relief that even when the law is not on our side, Karma is. "

XVII

Suddenly, there was silence between us, and it was difficult for me to understand, lest my talk hurt her hard. I even did not utter a single word out of my mouth. By this time, the train was almost vacant. I also started packing my things as my station was also arriving in an hour. But I was surprised to see *Jaya* as she was sitting next to the window looking out of it. It was a bright, sunny day and sun rays were entering through the window, passing through her eyes, but I could see that she was lost in her thoughts, not even blinking.

As I sat back on my seat opposite to her, after putting my things back in my bag, I heard her say *"Raja"*. I was surprised when she called my name for the first time, and I wasn't sure if she had called my name or if it was a hallucination because we were so busy talking that we didn't sleep the entire night. I glanced at her to confirm whether she called me or not and heard her say my name again. I replied to her, "Yes, tell me *Jaya.*"

Looking out of the window, she asked me, "When we are so proud of the way we are protecting our daughters, don't you think we equally need to protect India's son? The criminal mindset is not gender-biased. Why is it not hitting anyone's thoughts? So, why does the gender-biased law exists? Why do girl and her parents pretend to be idealists while just post-marriage they change their colour and start accusing the groom and his family of being orthodox even though if they are not? Why do they start hating the groom's side for whatever they say, even if they are polite? Why do they start misinterpreting them for every word? I was never aware that men were also subjected to violence. It was kind of an eye-opener for me. I am surprised to know the other half of the world, which was not known to me before. I was living in the world blindfolded. I believed what I listened to. But there is a lot of inconclusiveness. Our brother and father too belong to the same category of 'MEN'. If self-defense is a birthright, it is equal for both genders.

Whether a leaf falls on a thorn or a thorn falls on the leaf, the thorn will always be blamed. Similarly, whether men exploit women or women exploit men, the one who is always to be blamed is the male community. Nobody will ever try to change the angle and look at the other side of the coin, now that women have begun to use the law to harass men, which was originally intended to protect them. It's high time to discriminate against genders, from men and women, to good people and bad people despite gender. I am really surprised. Where is our government? Where is the legal body? Why are they not acting on it even though they sense the severity of this issue? As you said to me earlier, the court has acquitted the men who were not guilty but were trapped in the false cases. So, if they are the ones to give judgment, then I am sure they must be well versed with the situation."

Observing the never-ending curiosity in her, I thought to converse and calm her down. So, I started, "I am glad that you are being so thoughtful, but this change of thought should happen in every individual. True men should come out of their comfort zones and speak against the violence and injustice happening to them, and learn to fight for themselves. If you will not stand for yourself, then who else will? You need to shout out to the world to inform them about the agony that you are going through. A mom also feeds her kid when he/ she cries out loud.

Every man is vulnerable, and the law can be easily misused to make you suffer. As men are proud to bear the flag of feminism, even women need to think of their brothers and other male members of their family and should start bearing the flag of meninism and try to protect them. If women are no less than men, then why should boys only protect women? It's high time that we men need the support from women to get justice. As well said by Swami Vivekanand, "Society needs both men and women to function, develop, and progress. It is impossible for a bird to fly with only one wing." Therefore, men are equally important to a strong society as well. If we look through the prism of gender equality, both men and women will be found equally culpable.

Instead of bridging the gap between the genders, feminism is screwing up the lives of men and their whole families by utilising the advantage of so-called 'new found freedom.' It is being used mainly for extracting alimony. There is a new concept in town: harassing the innocent. So the only way to get justice is to harass the opponent, forcing them to come to the bargaining table and close the case by making the other party rich and satisfied. I was even surprised that the women claim that they get beaten up by their spouse, and then they file a case, and everything ends once they get a hefty amount. The amount of money balances out their irrational inner aggression and the case gets closed.

During childhood, we were beaten up to excel in our studies so that we could have a good future for ourselves. Now, history is repeating itself and we are being beaten up by the wife for a good package which we are earning through our education in the name of maintenance and alimony. I can't see a good future ahead as the maximum amount of my salary will go to the culprits without any fault of mine. If she had wanted the money, I would have given everything to her as she was my wife, but they need everything in life, freedom and money, as somehow they feel suffocated in a matrimonial relationship. Isn't alimony taking the place of dowry? I feel alimony is another name for dowry, as the purpose of both is extortion of money. When the legal body has taken a step against dowry, they should even do something for alimony as well. As it is becoming a criminal act by the bride and her family, they give away their daughters to us as they find us suitable for them, and the suitability check nowadays mainly depends upon the pay package.

There is terrorism, and the next big thing upcoming is 'female terrorism'. Their accusations against men are like gunshots. The bullet struck, and the person is gone forever. I am not a misogynist. I have my sister and mother. I respect every girl. But I believe in supporting the right and standing against the culprit regardless of gender. And I strongly believe that an individualistic or gender neutrality approach may help in punishing the really guilty, as justice should have no gender bias.

It's need of the hour to change the archaic patriarchal mindset, or else it will not be long before the groom is seen crying in their marriage rituals rather than the bride, contemplating leaving his parents, getting false cases, and losing a large sum of money.

Well, the Supreme Court has also in effect accepted that women tend to over-hype their personal grievances and may rope in all the family members of the groom. The problem which lies here is the low conviction rate in these cases, which is also fanning the fire that women may cry wolf as per their convenience. And you know what, the worst part here is that we men, after getting entangled in false cases, are made 'guilty until proven innocent' rather than looking into today's situation where the rate of false cases is increasing. The law should start thinking about changing it to 'innocent until proven guilty.' Maybe for the girl, it is merely a way to satisfy her ego, and for the law, it might be another case, but for the boy, it is his whole life getting ruined. Everyone existing in the world knows how much effort it takes to build and maintain a personal image. There is a struggle in every step, and to get over it with your dignity intact is not an easy task. But for a girl, it hardly takes a phone call to the cops or a case in court to ruin the life of a guy. The only measure to stop the false cases will be to work towards the rigorous prosecution of all the fake cases and pieces of evidence together with the wrong investigations carried out by the police. I would like to say that, "IT IS A BIG LIE, THAT REAL MEN DON'T CRY."

Tears started falling off my eyes. Maybe these were the tears that were hidden deep inside me under the name of masculinity. Maybe these were the tears that I was holding under the cover of a fake smile just to show my strength in front of my parents and sisters so that they wouldn't get distressed seeing me upset. This was the long hidden pain in me which I had held onto for a long time and was walking through the different phases of life pretending to be strong. But the truth was, I was all shattered inside, managing to look in one piece to the rest of society.

Trying to survive is similar to an ostrich who buries their head in the sand, assuming that if they can't see predators, the predators can't even see them. I am surviving with a feeling of shame to stand and face society, but the fact is that we can't survive without the people around us, and the people will not let us survive either. So, I chose to live like an ostrich, doing my daily tasks with my eyes closed, assuming as if no one was watching over me. I have learnt to live in denial of the existence of society around me just because I can't commit suicide as I have my older parents to take care of and don't even want to end my life without proving myself right to everybody who has considered me wrong or to the society that has accepted the fake charges that were put upon me. I need to prove my innocence to society before I die.

Disrupting the unending thoughts, *Jaya* said, "If this situation continues to progress, soon, only two genders will be left."

I interrupted her with a witty remark, "Hey, there are only two genders."

But she did not pay much attention to my words and continued saying, in a serious voice, "Yes, two genders. One will be FEMALE and the other will be FEW MALE, or there will be either WOMEN or NO MEN."

Her sentence gave me goosebumps. Maybe she is true.

She further continued, saying, "When feminism 1s never considered as female domination, then why is patriarchy considered as male domination, when we come across a female who uses feminism as a weapon to satisfy her personal ego in society? It's true that in the early days when women were restricted to the four walls of their homes, they were not satisfied and fought for the right to gain liberty, and it is very obvious for any gender to fight for equality until it is not misused to harm the opposite sex. But now, due to the positive societal changes that have taken place all over the world, the condition of women is far better than it used to be and is still improving.

It is really surprising to see how compassionate women have turned into revengeful souls or vindictives, misusing the privileges provided to them and using them as a double sword to slit the throats of the innocent opposite sex and making their lives miserable with their never-satisfied attitude, trying to satisfy their internal ego. There is a hidden strong message in everything for every daughter-in-law who is misusing the law: 'You are feeding the demon which may revert back to you and may harass you ten times more when you become a mother-in law.' Nobody benefits from matrimonial discord except the police, advocates, and associated arbitrators. I am not asking women to raise their voices for men. Instead, raise your voice for your own sake before it starts engulfing you in itself. Nobody knows what's in your store for the next few years. Now you must be enjoying the privileges as a daughter-in-law, but don't forget that the effectiveness of the law depends on the situation or on which role you are playing."

I further added, "If you are a mother to a daughter, you may feel that the laws are good and in favour for screwing up a boy, his relatives, or his family, but if you are a mother to a son, the same laws will look like an eagle's claws. The lawmaker has to do justice to the innocent and punish only the culprit. In so many matrimonial cases, I have never seen the bride or her family getting punished for wasting the court's time by putting forth false cases. Rather, they benefit from the alimony amount even if they are not able to prove any charges against the groom. If the groom is found guilty, he should be punished. If the bride and her family members are found guilty of faking up the cases to ruin the boy's societal image and extort money, they should all be equally punished and imprisoned. I am sure if little changes are made, the number of fake cases being reported will reduce. This should be made into a public movement to get the rights against injustice."

Our station had arrived and I was about to get down. I bent to pick up my luggage and turned to say goodbye, but to my surprise, she was still sitting on the berth looking outside and was in no hurry to pick up her luggage and get off the train. Her chirpiness was lost in her thoughts. Her happiness on getting engaged and soon to be married vanished somewhere. I turned to her and told her, "It was nice meeting you. You gave me a good company. Goodbye and good luck for your future endeavours."

Instead of greeting me goodbye, she bowed down, picked up her luggage, and said, "I am afraid to create any connection of cord with a male child in my womb ever in my life as it will be an indication of the sufferings for not just him but for the one whoever is related to him too. Moreover, I want my old age to be peaceful. God, please don't ever give me a male child. I am not as strong as *Raja* and his parents."

And she got off the train, making me numb and hard to move with her sentences, which gave me goosebumps. I could see her getting down and vanishing into the crowd on the platform.

www.ingramcontent.com/pod-product-compliance
Lightning Source LLC
Chambersburg PA
CBHW022020150726

47990CB00002B/745